Effective
Church
Finances

Effective Church Finances

Fund-Raising and Budgeting for Church Leaders

Kennon L. Callahan

HarperSanFrancisco

A Division of HarperCollinsPublishers

FIRST EDITION

Library of Congress Cataloging-in-Publication Data
Callahan, Kennon L.
    Effective church finances : budgeting and fund-raising for church leaders / Kennon L. Callahan. — 1st ed.
        p.   cm.
    Includes index.
    ISBN 0-06-061288-6 (alk. paper)
    1. Christian giving.   2. Church fund raising. I. Title.
BV772.C53   1992
254.8—dc20   91-59051
                                                            CIP

      94 95 96 RRD(H) 10 9 8 7 6 5 4 3 2

This work is dedicated to
our many friends
who are church business administrators,
financial secretaries, and church treasurers.
Their work means much in advancing God's mission.
                    —*Kennon and Julie Callahan*

Contents

Contents

Preface

This book shares practical suggestions, insights, and wisdom for effective church finances. It is for you, your workers, committee members, chairpersons, staff, and leaders. Invite all of them to study the book in study sessions or in a retreat setting. Include as many people as possible in your study.

In healthy congregations, all of the leaders and workers, not just the finance committee, understand effective budgeting and fund-raising. Frequently, the program council and the finance committee together give joint leadership to a study of the book for all people on committees, task forces, and mission teams in the congregation.

The suggestions in this book will help you and your congregation develop effective practices of budgeting and giving development. These practices will help you and your congregation to grow forward your giving.

I want to acknowledge and thank my many good friends who serve as church administrators, financial secretaries, fund-raisers, treasurers, bookkeepers, finance leaders, and pastors. They have contributed much to my understanding of budgeting and fund-raising.

I want to thank Julie McCoy Callahan. Her wisdom, spirit, and direct contributions have advanced this book substantively. It is an extraordinary experience to work and share together.

I want to thank John Shopp, senior editor at HarperSanFrancisco. John and I have worked well together as a team for many years. He has advanced my understanding of the art of writing. His insights and editorial wisdom have contributed greatly to the completion of this book.

Hilary Vartanian and Terri Goff have made numerous solid advances to the book. I am most grateful for the team of people with whom I work at HarperSanFrancisco.

I want to express my thanks to Dwayne Roberts, who typed the original manuscript and has contributed to the revisions that followed. She has contributed greatly to bringing the book into being.

May this book help you and your congregation in your mission. May the grace and peace of God be with you.

PART ONE

Developing Your Budget

Chapter 1

A Mission Budget

Effective church finances will advance your mission. Effective practices in church finances will strengthen the health of your congregation. These practices will grow forward your giving and the giving of your people.

Congregations who practice effective church finances have a stronger mission, help more people, and raise more money. Their mission is increased. Congregations that do not practice effective church finances find that their mission is weaker, they help fewer people, and they raise less money. Their mission is diminished.

Congregations invest considerable time, energy, and effort in church finances. When they utilize effective church finance practices, they invest less time, find more creativity, and have stronger results. They are, therefore, able to devote their primary time, energy, and effort to mission.

When congregations do not practice effective church finances, they invest too much time and have weaker results. They are not, therefore, able to give their best effort to mission.

People with a passion for mission are motivated to learn effective church finance practices. One of the stumbling blocks to mission is, "We don't have enough money." The importance of mission should not be deterred by the question of money. Practicing effective church finances puts your congregation in the best position to move forward in mission.

Effective church finance includes the following four areas. Each will help your mission and your future. Study these areas. Implement them. Each area is covered in depth in a section of the book.

1. Develop a strong mission budget.
2. Raise the giving of your congregation.
3. Set solid giving goals.
4. Grow your giving.

Giving is living. When we give, we come alive. As we give our best, we live our best. The purpose of life is giving. Many congregations help people to discover their gift for generosity. The four areas for effective church finances help people to grow their capacity for giving.

Developing a strong budget is the first area of effective church finances. Strong, solid budgets create strong giving. Weak budgets create weak giving. Base your budget on your major priorities. Help it to be a budget of wise investments for mission. A mission budget advances giving.

Three major categories of budgets are employed by congregations:

- a mission budget
- an organizational budget
- a cost budget

The most compelling and effective of the three is the mission budget. It includes several important qualities.

First, the mission budget is built on the major priorities of the congregation for the coming year. The congregation's long-range planning has developed these major priorities. Generally, effective congregations have no more than three to five major priorities at a time.

Second, for each of its major priorities, the mission budget includes only a few key objectives. The mission budget takes seriously the 20/80 principle:

20 percent of the things a grouping does delivers 80 percent of its results.

80 percent of the things a grouping does delivers 20 percent of its results.

Thus, a mission budget is clear on the 20-percenters to be accomplished in the coming year. These few key objectives are central to the mission budget.

Third, the mission budget is a people budget. People give money to people. A mission budget includes a focus on the people who will be helped through the congregation's major priorities. A mission budget also has a clear sense of the people who will be helping with each major priority and the leaders who will advance the overall mission.

Fourth, a mission budget is built on wisdom, judgment, vision, common sense, and prayer. A mission budget does not try to include every detail for the coming year. A mission budget takes seriously the few major priorities and key objectives that are important to achieve in the coming year. A mission budget works smarter, not harder.

You will note that I keep saying "a few" key objectives. A major priority may have from two to four key objectives related to it. Occasionally, a major priority may have four to six key objectives. It takes only a few 20-percenter key objectives to accomplish a major priority.

One of the mistakes some congregations make is to have too many major priorities. Another mistake is to have too many key objectives for each major priority. The mission budget centers on the 20-percenters.

The purpose of a giving campaign is to help people grow forward the generosity of their giving, not to raise a detailed, line-item budget. It is not necessary—indeed, it is not always useful—to have the total budget decided completely and exactly before having a giving campaign. Many congregations have their giving campaign before deciding their detailed budget for the coming year.

The congregations who do this most effectively are the ones who know their few major priorities and related key objectives. They invite people to give generously to these major priorities in mission. Having had a constructive giving campaign, they then decide a strong mission budget.

The congregations who do not know their major priorities have greater difficulty having their giving campaign before deciding their budget. They are not clear enough on where they are headed for people to know how best to help.

	Yes	No
The budget lives out a compelling compassion for mission.	___	___
The major priorities for the coming year are clearly stated in the budget plan.	___	___
The few key objectives for each major priority have been wisely selected; they are 20-percenters.	___	___
The people who will be helped will benefit from constructive mission.	___	___
The people who will be helping have the competencies and the compassion to share concrete, effective help.	___	___
The leaders who will advance the overall mission bring a sense of wisdom and vision, competencies and compassion to the overall mission of the congregation.	___	___

Table 1: A Mission Budget

The solution is not, therefore, to create an exact, detailed line-item budget prior to having a giving campaign. The wise solution is to decide the few major priorities for mission, have a constructive giving campaign, and then decide the full mission budget for the coming year.

Table 1 will help you to discover the ways in which your congregation's budget includes the characteristics of a mission budget.

A budget that matches these qualities is a strong, compelling mission budget. It will grow the mission. It will grow the giving.

The second type of budget, an organizational budget, is less compelling. Most commonly, this kind of budget is organized according to the committees of the congregation. If you look at this budget you can see the organizational chart of the congregation. Its organizing principle is based on grouping together the line items for which each committee is responsible and over which each committee has control.

Whenever the grassroots do not develop the congregation's major priorities, whenever the priorities and budget are developed primarily by the committees of that congregation, then what usually shows up is an organizational, institutional budget. Sometimes only a few people on a few committees develop the budget.

This type of budget is usually built on the following principle of scarcity:

> A few people on a few committees see only a few resources.

Since they are a few of a few, the budget they draw up is an allocation of those few available resources that they meagerly anticipate for the coming year. Sometimes the principle of control is also lurking in the background. A few people "know what is best" for the congregation, and those few people find ways to control the money.

An organizational, institutional budget has power and value for the people who participate in the committees. Churches with this type of budget raise the major portion of their giving from among the people who are, have recently been, or look forward to being on the committees of that congregation. The focus of the budget is on the organizational, institutional welfare of that local church.

The third type of budget, the cost budget, is even less compelling. Frequently, the cost, maintenance budget has these categories, usually listed in this order, and they seldom change from one year to the next:

- space and facilities costs
- denominational costs
- personnel costs
- program costs

This type of budget is usually drawn up by leaders who have pulled back into a conserving, holding, protecting, and preserving mentality. Using this kind of budget is not a practice of effective church finance.

Congregational leaders who use this kind of budget have not yet advanced their understanding of giving and stewardship. They have not grown the six principles for giving. They have yet to understand the motivational resources for giving. They do not practice positive reinforcement. Therefore, they have not raised the money that is generously available to be given.

This budget type is usually a symptom of leaders who—in a reactive, passive, cost-centered way—have taken a last fortress stance. But, a cost, maintenance budget is not a compelling source for giving. It raises just enough to get by year after year, almost but not enough. It misses all of the monies that could be generously given.

You will recognize this type of budget when you hear it explained on the Sunday morning just before Loyalty Sunday. Someone usually says:

> We want you to know that it costs X number of dollars per day just to keep the doors open, the lights on, and the utility bills paid.

Sometimes, that same person will go on to say:

> If you only realized how much it costs each day just to keep the doors of this church open, you would be more committed in your giving.

These statements only remind people of how much it costs them to keep their own lights on and their own utility bills paid. These are not compelling pictures with which to help people grow forward the generosity of their giving.

These statements distract people from Whose they really are. The focus is on scarcity. These statements look at life in terms of costs. People are not drawn to a cost-centered perception of life; instead, they are drawn to a mission-centered understanding of life. We live life best in our giving, not our conserving. We live life best in our service, not our survival.

Keep your mission budget simple. Most people are not interested in the budget detail of three hundred line items, carefully and precisely listing each individual dollar amount. People do have a primary interest in the major priorities and key objectives. Share these in as few words as possible. Provide word pictures; provide people pictures of the mission. Five to eight major pictures help. Share summary dollar figures for the major priorities and key objectives.

Feel free to have a detailed budget for accounting purposes and to make it available to anyone who is interested. You can say:

> We have copies available. Phone the church; we will mail you a copy of our line-item budget. It is an open document. We look forward to sharing it. Count on and depend on that it has been examined in depth by the appropriate committees and people.

With each copy of the line-item budget, include the one page that describes the major mission priorities toward which you are headed. Help people to see the forest as well as the trees.

Use your best creativity and wisdom. Adapt your present budget to a mission budget. Your mission budget will be distinctive from other congregations' mission budgets. The art is not so much to copy what someone else has done as to tailor-make your mission budget with your congregation. Help it to be simple and compassionate, sharing the mission for the coming year.

Plan your budget. Budget your plan. Live out your plan in your budget. A mission budget grows out of the grassroots development of the congregation's long-range plan. Involve as many people as possible in your annual, congregational long-range planning session. Grassroots development of the plan yields grassroots ownership for the giving.

Many congregations do solid long-range planning. They develop creative major priorities and key objectives. However, when the giving campaign arrives, some congregations fall back on an organizational budget or a cost budget.

Live out, consistently, your long-range plan in both your budgeting and your giving campaigns. Plan your work; work your plan. Plan your budget; budget your plan.

People share their giving generously through a mission budget. They are not motivated to share their giving through an organizational budget or a cost budget. To grow the giving of your congregation, develop a strong mission budget.

Chapter 2

Major Priorities

People give generously to major priorities. Mission congregations have a clear sense of their major priorities. They have an effective long-range plan for mission. They know which of the twelve central characteristics of effective churches (listed in Table 2) are their expands and adds for the coming year.

Relational	*Functional*
1. Specific, Concrete Mission Objectives	7. Several Competent Programs and Activities
2. Pastoral/Lay Visitation in the Community	8. Open Accessibility
3. Corporate, Dynamic Worship	9. High Visibility
4. Significant Relational Groupings	10. Adequate Parking, Land, and Landscaping
5. Strong Leadership Resources	11. Adequate Space and Facilities
6. Solid, Participatory Decision Making	12. Solid Financial Resources

Table 2: The Twelve Keys

First, build on your strengths. Do better what you do best. Expand certain current strengths. An *expand* is a central characteristic rated as an 8 on a scale of 1 to 10. The congregation plans to grow forward this strength to a 9 or 10. An expand is successfully grown forward by achieving the best two to four key objectives (the 20-percenters) that advance that strength.

Second, add new strengths to overcome current weaknesses. An *add* is a central characteristic rated between 1 and 7 on a scale of 1 to 10. The congregation plans to add it as a newfound strength, overcoming a current weakness or shortcoming. An add is successfully grown forward to a rating of 8 by achieving four to six key objectives.

Third, build your mission budget on the foundation of your long-range plan of expands and adds. Organize your budget in relation to these major priorities. Embody in your budget the central characteristics you are planning to expand and add during the coming year. You can describe how these expands or adds will help you to be in mission with this range of people—and the ways in which you plan to help.

Effective mission congregations do not try to strengthen all twelve characteristics each year. Their long-range plan for mission describes which specific characteristics are their major priorities for each of the coming four years. From this, they know which characteristics they plan to strengthen during the coming year.

Practice budgeting by objectives. Organize your mission budget around the central characteristics that are your major priorities. Let these priorities be the organizing principle around which the budget is developed. State the few key 20-percenter objectives you plan to accomplish to advance these priorities. Then describe the funding that will help achieve these objectives.

Specific, concrete mission objectives may be a major priority for the coming year. Describe the key 20-percenter objectives you plan to achieve. Develop a holistic, integrative, dynamic understanding of mission. People are interested in and support mission objectives.

You may have decided to add pastoral and lay visitation in the community as a newfound strength during the coming year. Gather into one major budget section the items that directly and indirectly will be helpful in achieving this major priority.

The characteristic of corporate, dynamic worship may be a major priority for the coming year. State the few key 20-percenter objectives regarding dynamic worship that you plan to achieve. Describe these objectives and the funding that will be helpful.

A major priority for the coming year may be to expand the current strength of significant relational groupings. One major section of your mission budget would include the key objectives that will contribute significantly to accomplishing this priority.

The central characteristics that shape your budget may develop from one year to the next. That is fine. The routine listing of the detailed line items year after year has the effect of producing mind-dulling complacency. When you organize the budget into the major central characteristic priorities for the coming year, you provide a compelling sense of urgency of what you are about on behalf of God's mission.

People give money to people. Describe who will be helped through your priorities. Once you have in place the priorities for the coming year, link them to the people who will be helped. It is not sufficient to say that we have "this priority in our children's program."

Share the range of people and the specific groupings of children and their families with whom you plan to be particularly helpful in the coming year, given the funds you seek. Share several pictures of who will be helped. When congregations are specific as to who will be helped through their giving, people respond generously and graciously.

Likewise, in describing your mission budget, describe the people who will be doing the helping. In a priority that focuses on reaching children and their families, share the people who will be helping with this outreach in your community. This will help develop a sense of mutual trust, respect, credibility, and confidence in the mission. Even though givers may not be familiar with the people who will be helped, they know and have confidence in the people who are sharing the help.

Further, share the leadership team who have helped in developing the long-range plan and who will give leadership in advancing the overall mission plan. Include the names of all people who have participated in the long-range planning sessions in which the major mission priorities were developed.

People give money to mission, not maintenance. Describe the major priorities in terms of the specific key objectives that will be helpful in people's lives and destinies. You will help people to discover deeply and richly the generosity of their giving.

Describe your major priorities as:

Services we plan to share in mission

Let the spirit of your mission budget be:

We plan to share these services with people in our congregation, in our community, in our country, and across the world.

Do not describe your major priorities as "services we are providing to you as a consumer—and therefore, will you please support the budget?" Say, rather, "These are the services that we, as a congregation, are supporting as wise investments in people's lives."

Yes, there is a sense in which we are consumers. And yes, we have an interest in the services we directly consume—even in our local congregation. And yes, therefore we will support a budget in relation to those services we plan to consume. However, that perspective shortchanges our true nature as God's children. We are finally people who are interested in helping. We finally want to be a part of a congregation that is sharing mission services because of Whose we are.

Look and plan four years ahead. A budget typically has an annual focus. Develop a forward-looking perspective with your budget. Help people to see that you are looking four years ahead, not focusing on only the current year.

You can do this in a simple way. Along with any copy of your annual mission budget, include one page that sets forth your long-range plan of major priorities. Show the central characteristics you plan to expand and add in each of the coming four years. Keep before your people a simple listing of the few key objectives related to each major priority.

This is most helpful during your giving campaign. People can see how their giving builds for the future. They can see how their gifts for this coming year will build the foundation on which to grow the mission achievements for the three years beyond.

Likewise, in meetings when the treasurer's report is distributed—whether monthly or quarterly—as a part of that report, include one page of major priorities, listing the central characteristics you plan to expand and add in the coming four years. Keep before people the long-range priorities toward which you are headed.

Even in a sport as simple as professional football, it takes at least five years to build a winning team. In something as complex as a mission of helping people with their lives and destinies, look at least four years ahead. Look at the current year and the three years yet to come. Look at least that far.

In summary, people share their giving generously through a mission budget of major long-range priorities. People are not motivated to share their giving through a routine annual budget. Grow the giving of your congregation. People give generously to major priorities for mission.

Chapter 3

Building an Investment Budget

A budget is a series of wise investments. The best way to think about your congregation's budget is as a series of wise investments on behalf of the mission to which God calls you in the world. The budget represents your investments in your congregation's present and future mission. Your investment budget has the purpose of helping people with their lives and destinies in the name of Christ.

When I suggest that your budget is a series of wise investments, I am not talking about how much interest your congregation is earning at the nearby bank. Do not think in terms of investing money in order to make money. I do not use the word *investments* in this fashion. Do not think about investing in stocks and bonds. That is not the kind of investments to which I refer.

I have in mind the understanding of investment in keeping with the original spirit of the root word. The word *investment* comes from the Latin verb *investire,* which means to clothe, to put clothes on. The verb is derived from *in* plus *vestes,* the latter meaning garment or clothing. The budget is the clothing we put on the mission.

To be sure, the mission teams supply the power and leadership for the mission—with God's help. At the same time, there is a genuine sense in which the budget—while not the essence or power of the mission—is the clothing we put on the mission. One can study the budget of a local congregation and know how it is clothing its mission for the coming year.

It is important to put away any notion that a budget is a plan for costs, expenses, or disbursements. In preparing this coming year's budget, the best question with which you can begin is:

> What will we invest on behalf of God's mission to help people with their lives and destinies?

The questions not to begin with are "What will be our costs during the coming year? What will be our expenses during the coming year? What will be our disbursements during the coming year?"

When we focus on costs, expenses, and disbursements, we only remind people of all their own costs in everyday, ordinary life. When people hear, "This is how much it costs to run our church during an average month," they think about how much it costs to run their family during an average month. You will neither advance the giving nor raise much money by reminding people how much it costs to run the church each month.

The best budgets are developed and put together prayerfully, generously, thoughtfully, and creatively. Develop your budget with prayer.

It is amazing to me that some finance committees, boards, pastors, and fund-raisers seldom pray as they develop the budget. They study last year's figures and this year's estimates. They project and prognosticate about the economy. They analyze the figures, the changes in the trends, and the analyses of their projections. Yet they do not pray. They do not live in Christ as they develop their budget.

Most of the finance committees, pastors, boards, and leaders with whom I have worked do pray—deeply and richly. They pray that God will give them wisdom and judgment, vision and common sense. They pray that God will help them to discern the mission to which God calls them in the year to come. Their prayer life is richly and fully a part of the planning for their mission, the development of their budget, and the raising of their money in their giving campaign.

Do not put forward an "exaggerated budget." This is a budget in which the leaders and pastor ask for more money than is really needed, thinking that they will fall short but that by exaggerating the goal they will end up with what they really need for the coming year. That is a travesty and lie. It is dishonest. It will cause the congregation never to believe their figures again.

When the congregation, the leaders, and the pastor trust in God in their prayer life, they do not need to fall back on the false gimmick of an exaggerated budget. The purpose of prayer is to discover God's guidance, not to support our own delusions of grandeur. A budget is generously, thoughtfully, and responsibly put together. A budget developed in prayer is an open, honest budget, not a hidden, exaggerated budget. The grassroots of the congregation tend to sense whether or not the finance committee, key leaders, and pastor have developed this budget in prayer.

There is some value in studying last year's figures and this year's estimates. Certainly there is some value in studying the trends in our congregations and in our culture. At the same time, however, there is no value in doing all of those things without also developing the budget in prayer.

God calls us to be stewards, not spenders. To focus on costs teaches people in your congregation to think of themselves not as stewards but as spenders. Stewards invest generously and wisely in fulfilling the mission to which God calls us.

Spenders, regrettably, spend money as though it were growing on trees and going out of style and then become distressed over their excesses. Or spenders become preoccupied with costs and turn into conserving, holding, protecting, and preserving people to keep the costs low.

When you really want to think in terms of costs, think of human costs. Ask:

> What is it costing our families, our community, by not having a strong youth program—by not helping some fifty to a hundred youth with their lives and destinies during this coming year?

Ask:

> What are the costs of not having worship that draws and is helpful to families with preschool children?

Ask:

What it is costing in human lives to not share our mission generously across the planet?

These are human-life costs, not dollar-and-cent costs.

When you measure costs, measure in lives, not light bulbs. Measure in people, not paper. Measure in mission, not mortar. Measure in help shared, not money conserved. When you think about "costs," think about all the people whose lives will not be richly helped with specific human hurts and hopes. Think about the human costs when we develop an attitude of conserving, holding, preserving, and protecting—only increasing the budget a marginal percent per year. What are the costs in your family, in your community, in the country, across the world?

In the best of family financial planning circles, a budget is clearly understood to be a matter of wise investments of our families' resources—so that we might have a whole and healthy family and live constructive lives. If in the world of family financial planning this constructive spirit prevails, we can help to put away the old focus on costs, expenses, and disbursements to which some have clung for far too long.

The words we choose indicate the theology we hold. When you are preparing the budget for the coming year, list the various line items in your budget in a column labeled "Investment Line Item." Table 3 shows an example of this.

By doing this, you create the consciousness that each line item in the budget is an investment. When we plan to invest $600 for church

Investment Line Item	Coming Year
Church School Literature	$600
Vacation Bible School	$200

Table 3: Mission Investment Budget

school literature during the coming year, we are investing it in the lives of our members, constituents, and people served in mission—children, youth, and adults.

When we have a line item for utilities—electricity, water, telephone, gas—we can no longer afford to think of it as the costs to keep the doors of this church open each year. Rather, we are investing in that line item for a gathering space—so that the congregation can gather in God's name to advance and grow their competencies to be mission teams in the world. Our best gatherings, task forces, and committee meetings will do solid work "in the locker room," inside the building, so that they can serve well "on the playing field," in the world—in God's mission.

With an investment budget, the treasurer shares a report conveying the spirit, the perspective, and the conviction that we have been investing our money on behalf of God's mission—for our families, our community, our country, and the world. This is not a report of what was spent. This is not what our costs were. This is not what our disbursements were this past month. This is our investments report. This is what we invested during this last month. Give up the old accounting term *disbursements*. Entitle the report "Investments."

There will be a period of transition for one or two treasurer's reports. Occasionally, someone may ask, "Why can't we just call it disbursements? That's what we've always known." Indeed, in declining churches and dying churches, leaders have become preoccupied with costs, expenses, and disbursements. We need a new preoccupation with investments in God's mission. It is more than a change of terms. It is a definitive, theological perspective as to Whose we are and what we are about.

This further counsel in relation to the treasurer's report: schedule the report near the end of the meeting of the finance committee or board. Regrettably, the custom in some congregations is that the meeting is called to order and opened with prayer, the minutes of the last meeting are read or dispensed with, and then comes the treasurer's report. Having this report early in the meeting means that most subsequent decisions are made on the basis of whether we think we have enough money or not.

I suggest the following sequence of events for the meeting and would certainly have the treasurer's report third from last:

- Open with prayer.
- Distribute the minutes.
- Share whose lives have been helped since we last met.
- Decide the key decisions that will advance the mission and the people we plan to help during coming time.
- Give the treasurer's report of our mission investments.
- Have a shepherding word from a key leader or our pastor.
- Close with prayer.

With the treasurer's report third from last in the meeting, the treasurer now reports on the ways in which the "clothing of our mission" has lived itself out as wise investments since we last met.

The best treasurer's report shares:

- "how much has been given to support the mission," not "how much income was received"
- "how much was invested in the mission," not "what was spent"

Look at the report through the eyes of the givers. The report is more than how much income was received, what the costs were this past month, and whether we ended up in the black or the red.

Report on the contributions given and the investments shared. In this fashion, the budget again and again, month by month, is reinforced as a series of wise investments. The budget shares this congregation's generosity to advance God's mission—in helping people with their lives and destinies.

People share their giving generously through a mission budget of wise investments. People are not motivated to share their faith thorough a budget of costs, expenses, or disbursements. Grow the giving of your congregation. Grow the strong, competent practice that your congregation builds an excellent investment budget.

PART TWO

Raising Your Giving

Chapter 4

Giving Campaigns

Raising your giving is the second area that will help your congregation to have effective church finances. Giving development is the long-term growth of the generosity of people in your congregation. A specific fund-raising campaign may be part of your long-term giving development plan. Yet giving development is more than fund-raising.

Dudley Hafner of the American Heart Association and Peter Drucker, a highly respected, longtime consultant, suggest the term *fund development* rather than *fund-raising*. They rightly observe that fund development is really people development. The task is developing both the givers and the volunteer leaders who advance the giving.

In reflecting on their discussion, I have come to the term *giving development*. The term *fund development* still looks at the activity through the eyes of the fund-raiser. What we are about is giving development. Look at the matter through the eyes of the giver instead of through the eyes of the fund-raiser. When you look through the giver's eyes, you see that we are seeking to help people grow their generosity. We are helping them to develop their giving. Thus, the better term is *giving development*.

Giving development is people development. The four areas of effective church finances focus on the qualities that help people to grow forward their generosity in their giving and in their life.

People give in many ways. Some share their generosity in steadfast, regular ways. Some give generously in short-term, highly intensive ways.

Some are solid marathon runners in their giving. Some are excellent sprinters. God blesses the giving of all.

Goals are the wings of vision. What raises the giving is the vision. The stronger the vision, the more generous people are. Once you have developed a strong mission budget, then have a constructive giving campaign.

A constructive giving campaign that includes the following five stages is in the best position to be successful:

- strategy objectives
- education
- motivation
- invitation
- follow-up

Developing solid strategy objectives is the first stage in a constructive giving campaign. Strategy objectives focus first on advancing the giving in the congregation and then on raising the annual budget. This is the proper order.

Decide your strategy objectives and then select a campaign approach that lives these out. The type of campaign you use from one year to the next is best determined by your strategy objectives. First, ask yourself:

What do we want to accomplish that will grow the giving in our congregation?

Then ask yourself:

What campaign method will best help?

Effective congregations plan their giving development in this sequence.

Congregations who have difficulty raising money usually have reversed the sequence. Indeed, such congregations hardly ask the first question. Their sole focus is on selecting a campaign method. Some continue to use a campaign method they have used for years, even though it has had a diminishing return. Others are drawn to whatever campaign method is the fad of the moment. Such congregations would do better by considering first their strategy objectives and then selecting the best campaign method to achieve that objective.

Listed below are four suggested strategy objectives you will find helpful. Each one will advance the giving of your congregation. Each has a distinctive focus:

- Increase the number of new giving and pledging households.

- Advance the number of workers and leaders who participate.

- Increase the giving of specific current giving and pledging households.

- Advance the congregation's giving a quantum leap.

Each of these strategy objectives is discussed in depth in the next chapter. For the moment, it is important to know that the first stage in a successful giving campaign is selecting the strategy objectives that will best advance the giving of your congregation.

An important word on timing will help. As best you can, make decisions about your strategy objectives during one of the best giving months in your congregation. All congregations have high-money months and low-money months of giving. Congregations do their best planning and make their best decisions on giving campaigns in months of stronger giving.

Try to avoid making decisions about your budget and your strategy objectives during a low-money month. Churches that decide their annual budget during a low-money month usually underbudget the potential mission that that congregation can accomplish in the coming year. Congregations that decide their strategy objectives in a low-giving month inevitably go for the quick fix rather than looking to the long haul of solid giving development.

Try not to conduct your giving campaign during a low-money month. Giving campaigns held in a low-money month usually raise less money. The campaign is surrounded by the quagmire of the sinking-ship mentality, struggling during the month of the campaign just to meet the current budget.

The question on the grapevine becomes "If we cannot meet this month's budget needs, how can we possibly raise the budget for the coming year?" Your giving pattern analysis (see Chapter 9) will show you the most promising high-giving months in which to decide your strategy objectives and to conduct your giving campaign.

It is worth noting that October in the northern hemisphere is a predictable low-money month in many congregations. People are catching up on bills for vacation expenses and going-back-to-school expenses that have shown up in credit-card statements at the end of September. Yet October has been a traditional month for conducting giving campaigns. That tradition can be traced back to the time of the harvest in a rural culture with a barter economy. While October may be your customary time, you may want to reconsider the timing in light of the giving pattern analysis of your congregation.

Education is the second stage in a constructive giving campaign. Educate your congregation on the following areas:

- the mission plan for the coming year—who will be helped, who will share the helping, and who has participated in developing the mission priorities

- the principles for giving

- the six sources for giving

- a theology of stewardship that is biblical and focuses on the stewardship of God's mission

You will find in-depth resources on these areas in my book *Giving and Stewardship in Effective Churches*. Many congregations are helped by a congregation-wide study of this book. Based on the pilgrimage of your congregation, you may, from one year to the next over a four-year period, focus more fully on one and then another of these educational emphases. Share all of them each year, rotating the predominant emphasis each year.

Be creative in the ways you carry out the educational stage. Consider all these possibilities and then select those that match best with your congregation:

- personal visits
- small-group gatherings
- large-group gatherings
- worship services
- personal phone calls
- short videotapes shared among the congregation
- short audiotapes
- personal notes
- personal letters
- brochures and booklets
- direct mail
- signs and banners

Draw on some of these educational possibilities to educate your congregation for the coming year's mission.

These possibilities for education are most helpful when shared with a spirit of compassion and a sense of community, when the focus is relational and personal rather than functional and institutional.

One of the best relational opportunities for education is in small-group or large-group gatherings. A small-group gathering might be a home meeting, possibly through existing relational groupings in your congregation, such as adult classes, circles, fellowship groups, or Bible study groups. These offer a strong relational dynamic for the education.

The focus is relational, on who we are as a group and how we can inform ourselves on our congregation's mission. The educational emphasis is not just institutional, not just on the functional budget goal for the coming year or on what's wrong with the church.

Large-group gatherings could include church dinners, town forums, and special events. In a large-group gathering we run the risk of losing the relational, person-centered dynamic of the small group. Thus, it becomes even more important to develop the spirit of compassion and sense of community vital to the educational process.

The service of worship is another time for an educational possibility. Sometimes a minute for mission is shared Sunday to Sunday over several weeks prior to the giving campaign. Sometimes the education is done across the year during certain services of worship. These are planned especially for the purpose of educating the congregation on the mission for the coming year.

The other educational possibilities are especially effective when they are shared with both the content and spirit of the motivational resources of compassion and community. Have a balance of these educational possibilities so that they mutually reinforce the message that you want to convey during a specific giving campaign. Develop a plan for the coming four years that draws on those educational possibilities that match best with your congregation.

Education is not motivation. The amount of time you invest in the educational stage of your giving campaign is important, yet many effective congregations can invest a relatively short period of time in the education stage. However, when you are planning to grow the congregation's giving by a quantum leap, the educational stage of the campaign might appropriately be for a slightly longer time.

Some congregations that have not raised their budget for many years may decide to invest a significant period of time in the education stage. They have a long-term, processive educational focus building toward the actual motivation and invitation stages of the campaign. It is a matter for your best wisdom and judgment. You want to invest enough time to be informative. You do not want to invest so much time as to create analysis paralysis, an excessive focus on analysis without action.

It is important to note that this is the time when you are delivering information and understanding. That is not the same as motivation. When you have done the education, you still need to do the motivation.

What you achieve in the education stage is the transmission of information and understanding. Be aware that information in and of itself is not motivation.

Motivation is the third stage in a constructive giving campaign. The importance and value of the motivation stage are decisive. Study Part Three, "The Motivations for Giving," in *Giving and Stewardship* for in-depth resources on the five major motivations out of which people give.

For now, it is important to note that giving campaigns based on compassion and community are more helpful in reaching the grassroots. If you seek primarily to advance the giving of key leaders, then a focus on commitment, reasonability, and challenge will resonate well with them. Keep in mind, however, that the grassroots do not respond well to messages of commitment and challenge. Compassion and community will resonate best with them.

Consider seriously the spirit of the congregation. Do the key leaders and grassroots have the spirit that "we are a winning cause"? Or is the spirit that "we are a sinking ship"? You will want to allow sufficient time for the motivational stage, depending on the prevailing spirit of the congregation.

You want to build sufficient motivation that people decide to grow forward the generosity of their giving, but you do not want to focus so long on motivation that the campaign passes its peak before you get to the invitation stage.

It is possible to combine education and motivation and to do those two stages simultaneously. The danger of combining the two stages is that leaders make the mistake of assuming that education is the same as motivation. Usually they will end up focusing on education and neglecting motivation.

For this reason, it is frequently more helpful to separate these stages. Decide first on your strategy objectives, then have an educational stage to your campaign, and then have a third stage of your campaign that is primarily and decisively motivation.

Invitation is the fourth stage in a constructive giving campaign. The invitation stage is when you confidently and assuredly invite people to decide to give generously to God's mission during the coming year. Have a confident closure invitation.

With a sense of assurance and peace, strength and calm, invite people to make their best decision to give generously to God's mission. This can be done without a quake or quiver in the voice. This can be done without hard pounding of the pulpit or sermons of dramatic legalism. People respond well to a confident, straightforward invitation.

Congregations most often falter at the invitation stage. They may become nervous, awkward, embarrassed. They may have been timid and uncertain for several years; then, to compensate and counterbalance that, they become hardnosed and overbearing.

Sometimes the finance committee will tell the pastor:

This year we want you to deliver two hard-hitting sermons on giving and stewardship. You have got to tell these people what they must do.

The finance committee acts like cheerleaders, telling the preacher, "Hit 'em again, hit 'em again, harder! Harder!" This kind of overcompensating tends to backlash.

Consistency works best. Faltering vacillation between the timid and the hardnosed approaches is not helpful. Have a strong, straightforward invitation each year. Share the invitation with compassion and community.

The more personal the invitation, the more generous the giving. Many successful congregations share the giving invitation through a personal invitation. Most often, this is done individually with each person or family. Occasionally, it is done in a small-group gathering. Who asks who is decisive. People grow forward their giving in the invitation. The quality of the invitation counts.

If your practice is to share the invitation during a Sunday service of worship, you will do better to have two consecutive Sundays of invitation. The tradition of having only one Sunday misses many people. Telling the worshipers, "If you can't be there on Pledge Sunday, be sure to bring your card the following Sunday" just makes all of those people who make their pledge on that second Sunday feel like "second-class citizens." Have two solid Invitation Sundays. Call them Mission Sundays, or Giving

Sundays, or Love Sundays, or Invitation Sundays, or Decision Sundays. Calling them Loyalty Sundays appeals primarily to longtime key leaders. It does not resonate with the grassroots. Give people two equally important opportunities to decide.

Set aside sufficient time for the invitation stage. Give people a genuine opportunity to make a decision. Some people come to a decision quickly. Some people come to a decision slowly. Do not rush the invitation stage.

Follow-up is the fifth stage in a constructive giving campaign. Some congregations do not decide to do any follow-up until after the invitation stage has been completed. They are working from the wrong premise. They think that if they raise the budget goal, then they won't need to do any follow-up. Their wishful thinking gets in the way of excellent planning.

The purpose of the giving campaign is to help people grow forward their giving. The follow-up stage gives people a second chance to advance their giving. The purpose of the follow-up stage is giving development, not budget raising. Decide how you plan to do the follow-up before you begin the giving campaign. The follow-up stage is equally as important and decisive as any of the other stages of your campaign. It is the time when you give people a second chance. It is the time when you are given the opportunity to do the clean-up work—to overcome whatever shortcomings and failures may have occurred during the campaign.

The follow-up stage may be brief, and yet it is decisive. It needs to be well planned and well done. Approach the follow-up personal contacts with the expectancy of making a new best friend, giving each one the courtesy and consideration you would extend to your best friend.

Both personal visits and personal phone calls are effective follow-up methods. Whether you visit in person or by phone, confidently and warmly invite the person to give to the church, affirming that their giving will help in the congregation's mission.

It is important to give people another chance. Lots of us are who we are because someone gave us a second chance. Indeed, some of us have needed third and fourth chances.

There is a biblical basis for giving a second chance. Remember that even at the end of three extraordinary years with Jesus, Peter still denied him three times. Yet Jesus declared that it was on the faith of Peter that the movement would be built forward. Paul was certainly given a rich, full second chance to live beyond the persecutions and legalisms of Saul. Plan for a solid follow-up stage in your giving campaign.

Accomplish well each of these giving campaign stages. Wherever objectives, education, motivation, invitation, and follow-up are solidly done, you are well on your way to advancing the giving of your congregation.

Education Stage: Major Emphases Long Range Plan

1. Select the educational emphasis that you can grow forward most easily in year 1. Check it in the column labeled "Year 1."

2. Decide which educational emphasis can be developed best for years 2, 3, and 4. Check them in the corresponding columns.

	Year 1	Year 2	Year 3	Year 4
The mission plan for the coming year—who will be helped, who will share the helping, and who has participated in developing the mission priorities				
The principles for giving				
The six sources for giving				
A theology of stewardship that is biblical and focuses on the stewardships of God's mission				

Each year, positively reinforce the educational emphases that you have well in place.

Educational Possibilities: Long-Range Plan

1. Select the educational possibilities that you can best grow forward in year 1. Check them in the column labeled "Year 1."

2. Decide which educational possibilities can be best developed for years 2, 3, and 4. Check them in the corresponding columns.

	Year 1	Year 2	Year 3	Year 4
Personal visits				
Small-group gatherings				
Large-group gatherings				
Worship services				
Personal phone calls				
Short videotapes				
Short audiotapes				
Personal notes				
Personal letters				
Brochures and booklets				
Direct mail				
Signs and banners				

Each year, positively reinforce the educational possibilities that you have well in place.

Chapter 5

===

Campaign Strategy Objectives

Constructive giving campaigns are built on a foundation of solid strategy objectives. Strategy strengthens success. Decide the strategy objectives that will best advance the giving of your congregation. Decide your strategy objectives before you choose a particular campaign methodology.

The best way to raise your budget is not to focus on raising the budget. Instead, focus on the strategy objectives that will raise the giving. The happy by-product is that you will also raise the budget.

Consider which of these distinctive strategy objectives is the best focus of a giving campaign in a specific year:

- Increase the number of new giving and pledging households.

- Advance the number of workers and leaders who participate.

- Increase the giving of specific current giving and pledging households.

- Advance the congregation's giving a quantum leap.

Plan four years ahead and choose one of these objectives as the major strategic priority for each of the coming four years.

You can sequence the first three strategy objectives in whatever order makes best sense. Tailor the timing to your congregation. Do those three in whatever order works best for your congregation.

Build the base in years 1, 2, and 3 toward a major advance in the congregation's giving in year 4. Thus, a four-year strategy plan might look like this:

Year 1: Our objective is to increase the number of new giving and pledging households by (*twenty*) percent.

Year 2: Our objective is to advance the number of workers and leaders who participate by (*thirty*) percent.

Year 3: Our objective is to increase the giving of specific current giving and pledging households—that is, helping (*twenty*) percent of our current giving households to increase their giving in major ways.

Year 4: Our objective is to advance the congregation's giving a quantum leap of (*forty*) percent.

In year 1, you broaden the base of giving households. In year 2, you broaden the base of participating households. In year 3, a significant percent of your giving households advance their giving in major ways. They set a new standard for generous giving.

With the broader base, the increased participation, and a story to share of the ways a significant portion of the congregation have grown their giving, you can help the congregation forward a quantum leap in giving in year 4.

The art is to lay the foundation so well in the first three years that the quantum-leap year is a natural and evolutionary development.

There are at least two things to avoid doing. First, it is a mistake to assure your congregation year after year that the coming year's budget is only a (*3.92*) percent increase, implying it is hardly keeping up with inflation. The church that does this for several years in a row will have allowed itself to fall behind in its mission work. This leads to two possible outcomes: either a need for an enormous catch-up to get back on track with its mission or a long, slow slide as the congregation declines over the years.

Second, avoid trying to produce a quantum leap every year. When you repeatedly attempt to have a major year, the congregation feels harassed.

This haranguing, year after year, has a significantly diminishing return.

Most importantly, I want you to see how the planned four-year development of these strategy objectives will help you to significantly grow the giving in your congregation. It is possible once every four years to achieve a major quantum leap.

The art is to develop a four-year strategy objective plan. Use wisdom and judgment in deciding the best sequence. Then choose a campaign approach that will best help you to achieve the major strategy objective for each year.

When you have well in place your four-year plan of strategy objectives, and you competently deliver the education, motivation, invitation, and follow-up stages, you can count on and depend upon, year after year, having solid, successful giving campaigns.

The first strategy objective is to increase the number of new giving and pledging households. Having this objective as your goal invites you to focus your campaign in a distinctive way.

The primary objective is not to raise the annual budget. That is a secondary, albeit important, objective. Instead, this strategy objective focuses primarily on the number of new giving or new pledging households that result from the campaign. The more new giving and pledging households you discover, the more likely—as a secondary, happy by-product—that you will also raise the annual budget goal.

The purpose is to broaden the base, increase the number of households who are supporting the mission of your congregation. The purpose is to help people "come on board" as new giving and pledging households—at whatever level of giving they can best manage. You are seeking to help them to begin giving to the mission.

You can focus on increasing the number of new giving households, counting on them to give generous recorded contributions during the coming year. Or you can focus on increasing the number of new pledging households, helping people to begin pledging generously. Or you can focus on both—helping people to become new giving or new pledging households.

As an example, you may have a hundred giving households in your congregation. Your campaign objective might be to discover twenty (or thirty) new giving households. A 20 (or 30) percent increase in giving households is substantial.

At the time you invite people to be workers and leaders in this campaign, you ask them to focus on helping people who are not now giving to become new giving and pledging households. The campaign report sessions primarily track the *number* of new giving and pledging households. To be sure, you will also track the total pledging amount, but workers are primarily encouraged to discover people who are not now giving and help them to come on board with their giving.

If you help a solid percentage of your potential giving households to come on board with the generosity of their giving, you will have a successful giving campaign. As a happy by-product, their net new giving will also help you to reach your annual giving goal.

There are four principal groups with which you could advance the number of new giving and pledging households:

- members who have joined during the current year
- members who have joined during the past three years
- worship participants
- active constituents

Think of these groups as potential giving households, not nongiving households. Mostly, it is a field rich unto the harvest. Yes, someone may have worked that field many times before. Yet it may have been done in hurried ways, not anticipating many results. The focus may have been on commitment and challenge—and you have found that does not work with the grassroots of the congregation. Now see them—and value them—for the potential giving households that they are.

The first grouping with which you can increase the number of new giving and pledging households is new members who have joined during the current year. In terms of giving, they are usually one of the neglected groups in local congregations.

The following objectives are helpful for a new-member orientation class:

Shepherding. Help new members discover the ways in which they can both benefit from and participate in the shepherding of the congregation.

Worship and spiritual growth. Help new members discover ways they can grow their prayer life, worship life, and understanding of the Christian mission.

Groupings. Help new members discover one significant relational group in which they will find a sense of roots, place, belonging, sharing, and caring.

Mission. Resource new members; do not recruit them. Help new members discover where they can best participate in God's mission. Do not help new members to "fill some vacant slot." Resource new members in ways that help them discover where their own strengths, gifts, and competencies can best be invested in God's mission.

Giving. Help new members confirm their giving with their pledge.

This last item is very precise. The classic mistake with new members is to have a functional orientation that focuses on the organizational structure and history of the church and gives the members a packet of all the programs and activities. Then someone says:

> By the way, included in your packet is a pledge card. You can fill it out whenever you want. Feel free to turn it in to the church office at some point in the future.

That awkward, embarrassed, tenuous way of inviting new members to confirm their giving does not work well. It teaches new members that they do not count. It does not take seriously that most new members have already been giving before they join—in loose plate and recorded contributions.

A better orientation describes the ongoing mission of the congregation, the objectives and people who are carrying out the mission, and then describes how the new members can help—through their participation and their continued giving. Invite them to prayerfully consider a pledge in an amount above their previous giving as they join in with the mission team.

Conduct new-member orientations with confidence and assurance. Invite new members' continued giving during the month in which they join.

The second grouping with which you can increase the number of new giving and pledging households is members who have joined during the past three years.

Look back over the three years prior to the current year and discover those new members who have yet to confirm their giving with their pledge. You may find that there are enough of these households that they could be a primary focus for your giving campaign.

A third grouping with which you can increase the number of new giving and pledging households is worship participants who are nonmembers. These people have evidenced an interest in your congregation's mission by worshiping with you. They are teaching you, more often than not, that if they have a church home, it is your congregation. This is true with your Christmas and Easter worship participants as well.

Do not hold it against these people that they are not members. Many people give generously to a cause in which they have confidence and yet are not members.

As you take seriously what the giving of these people can mean toward the mission, you teach them that you take seriously who they are and what their generosity can help achieve.

A fourth grouping with which you can increase the number of new giving and pledging households is active constituents. These are people who are not members and yet who participate in some program or activity in your congregation.

For whatever reasons, these people are finding a sense of help, hope, and home in some of your congregation's programs and activities. You may well decide that this is the year to encourage them to advance their participation with their giving.

Choose with which one or more of these four groups to focus. You may decide to focus with all four groups. You may discover yet another group with whom it would be helpful to focus. The purpose of this strategy objective is to increase the number of new giving and pledging households. The greater the number of new giving households, the more likely your congregation will have solid giving resources.

The second strategy objective is to advance the number of workers and leaders who participate. The purpose is to broaden the base of people who:

- plan for the mission

- develop the mission budget

- help to raise the money

The more workers and leaders who are involved in any of these three, the easier it will be to advance the generosity of your congregation.

Grassroots planning results in grassroots giving. Involve as many people as possible in planning the mission. Top-down planning results mainly in key leader giving. Whenever the planning for the coming year is done by a select few, then what you can count on and depend on is that generally a select few people will support the church's budget.

Twelve Keys Planning encourages churches to involve as many people as possible in the planning. The *Twelve Keys Planning Workbook* and the *Twelve Keys Leaders' Guide* are resources specifically designed to help you achieve grassroots planning. The more people involved in the planning, the larger the pool of excellent ideas and good suggestions that your congregation has available.

The more people involved in the planning, the greater the probability that wisdom, judgment, vision, common sense, and prayer will be present. Constructive and creative ways forward are more likely to be discovered. It is also true that the more people who are involved in the planning—the more grassroots ownership for the planning—the more likely it is that you will be successful in growing the generosity of your congregation.

A second way in which you can increase the base of people participating is in developing the mission budget. Involve as many people as possible in planning the mission, and then do not make the mistake of asking only the finance committee to develop the mission budget for the coming year.

Once you know the mission plan—the central characteristics you plan to expand and add and the few key objectives related to each for the coming year—then gather as many people as possible to develop what the budget will be. Look for excellent ideas and good suggestions that will create a wise, thoughtful budget. Include grassroots task forces, standing committees, commissions and boards, and elders and staff in developing a sound, solid budget.

Note that at this stage, you are not putting together a detailed, line-item budget, exact to the penny. What you want to achieve is a broadly based budget that will support the major priorities for the coming year. A more detailed budget can best be achieved after the conclusion of your giving campaign.

A third way in which you can involve people is advancing the number of workers and leaders who participate in the giving campaign. The more people who have good fun and good times participating in the giving campaign, the easier it is to raise money and the more it helps the campaign to be a major event of community. When you focus on the dynamics of community being shared together in the campaign, you are more likely to be successful.

There is a sense in which the strategy objective of advancing the workers and leaders who participate is the campaign before the campaign. That is, your giving campaign will be successful when you are successful in the preliminary participation campaign.

In one church, an estimated total of ninety people had been involved in one or more of the three areas mentioned above during the prior year. They decided to advance the number of workers and leaders involved in the coming year by 33 percent. That is, they decided to grow the number of workers and leaders from ninety to 120 people who would be involved in one of the three ways.

That meant helping ten new people to come on board in planning the mission, ten to come on board in developing the budget, and ten to come on board participating in the giving campaign. It was a simple, straightforward, successful goal. The happy by-product was that the giving of the congregation advanced as well.

The art of this strategy objective is to advance the number of workers and leaders. The greater the number of participating people, the more likely your congregation will have solid giving resources.

The third strategy objective is to increase the giving of specific current and pledging households. The purpose is to help people grow the depth and generosity of their giving. The more people who increase their giving, the more likely the congregation is to have the spirit of a growing and developing mission.

To implement this giving objective, focus primarily with three groups of people:

- people whose giving has remained the same for two or more years
- people who have decreased their giving during the current year
- people who have given in prior years and have not given in the current year

Consider first the grouping of people whose giving and/or pledge has remained the same for two or more years. With many households, there may be excellent reasons why their pledge and giving have remained the same.

Some people are on a fixed income, and their capacity to advance their giving is limited. There are people on fixed incomes, however, who are not yet giving at their very best and who could, in fact, grow their giving substantially. When you invite people to increase their giving, one group to focus on is those whose giving has remained the same for two or more years, whether or not they are on fixed incomes.

A second grouping includes those people who have decreased their giving during the current year. It may be particularly important to help these people to increase their giving back to the level of the prior year or to advance it beyond that level.

It is true that tragic events impact a family's well-being, and they simply may have to decrease their giving. It is true that in tough times some people lose their jobs and appropriately discontinue their giving.

It is also true that some people decrease their giving because the church is not meaning quite as much to them in their own lives as it used to. They are not angry and upset with the church. They are not planning to leave in a huff and a puff. But for whatever reasons—mission, shepherding, worship, significant relational groupings—the congregation has not maintained its meaningfulness in their lives in recent years, and they simply decide to decrease their giving.

It is important that the church fulfill its covenant with its members. This includes the delivery of mission, shepherding, worship and prayer, and active efforts to help people find their significant relational grouping. When a congregation fails to do these things, it is predictable that eventually people will decrease their giving. The solution is not to harangue these people to deepen their commitment. The solution is for the church to fulfill its covenant well with these people and then to encourage them to reconsider their giving.

The third grouping are those people who have a giving and/or pledging record in prior years, but have not given in the current year, for whatever reason. One might discover that there are simple reasons as to why this has happened. One might discover that they are still vitally interested in participating in the congregation.

We regrettably remember the few who left in a huff and a puff. We hardly notice the many who quietly slipped away. One can focus the resources and invitation of the campaign in such a way as to help people rediscover their own life mission and therefore their own participation in God's mission.

In this strategy objective, it does not help to harangue people that they "ought to be doing better" or "should do more." The art is to discover wherein among the three groups you can best lead people forward to a richer and fuller generosity of giving.

The fourth strategy objective is to advance the congregation's giving a quantum leap. People increase their giving in quantum leaps, not gradually. People who have been giving twenty dollars a month do not increase their giving the next year to twenty-one dollars, the next year twenty-two dollars, and so on. People giving twenty dollars a month continue giving at that amount for several years; then they decide to advance their giving to thirty dollars a month. Through their eyes that is a 50 percent increase in their giving. That is a quantum leap.

The first three strategy objectives will build the foundation for a quantum leap in the giving of your congregation. Accomplish those objectives in a solid manner; lay the foundation well. In the year you want to achieve a quantum leap in your congregation's giving, be sure to do these two things well:

- Develop a lean, generous budget.

- Focus on the groups most likely to help.

This will put you in a strong position to help the congregation grow forward its giving a quantum leap.

When you develop the budget, be certain it is lean—there is no waste; there is no fat; there are no hidden, miscellaneous line items. It is a bare-bones budget.

It is not true that the only time you should focus on having a lean budget is when you have to cut it. It is far more important to focus on a lean budget when you are growing the giving a quantum leap. It is precisely then when there should be no waste or extravagance.

It is a budget that is generous in mission. It is a creative, constructive budget that advances well the mission. New possibilities for mission are included. Each new item has integrity in relation to the budget. When you are increasing the giving a quantum leap, it is decisive to advance the mission in specific, concrete ways.

When I suggest that you focus on the groups most likely to help with the quantum leap, I am thinking of:

- major mission priorities

- shepherding

- active participation

- significant relational groupings

Consider inviting the people who are a major mission priority to grow forward their giving a quantum leap. If your congregation decides that a major mission priority is families with preschool children, have your best campaign workers and leaders be in direct personal contact with these families to help them advance their giving. Live out your mission in your giving campaign.

You might have decided that a major mission priority is people who are retired. Invest some of your best workers and leaders in contacting these people to advance their giving. Whatever your major mission priorities for the coming three to five years, help those groups with whom you are directly in mission to advance their giving.

Consider the people who have recently participated in the shepherding of the congregation. There will be families who have experienced the birth of a new child, families who have experienced the loss of a loved one, families who have been helped in this crisis or that tragedy, families with whom the church has celebrated good news—excellent events in their lives. Households that have experienced recent shepherding care are households with whom we, as best we can, have fulfilled some of our own covenant responsibilities. Consider, as well, which households recently have shared and participated in giving shepherding. These specific households would be among those you would invite to advance their giving.

We do the shepherding for the integrity of the shepherding. At the same time, many people decide to advance their giving because they have finally discovered what the church is really about through its shepherding.

Consider the households who actively participate in some program or activity of your congregation. They evidence by their participation that they are finding resources helpful in their lives and destinies. Focus particularly on those participating households who are involved in one of the major priorities of the congregation for the current and the coming years. Very frequently, they will be glad to help.

Consider the strong significant relational groupings in your congregation who deliver a sense of roots, place, belonging, sharing, and caring. You might want to focus with these households, and with those whose life situation matches well with these strong significant relational groups.

You will think of other possibilities for growing the giving of your congregation a quantum leap. Use your best wisdom to think through where best to focus your leadership, energies, efforts, and compassion.

I encourage you to develop a long-range plan of strategy objectives. What raises money is vision. The strategy objectives are handles for the vision.

Accomplish one major strategy objective for each year. Avoid repeating the same strategy objective year after year. That may be habitual and easy, but it has a marginal return. You lose out on all the new giving that will come to you with an effective plan of strategy objectives.

The greater the vision, the more likely the congregation will have solid giving resources.

Strategy Objectives: Long-Range Plan

1. Select the strategy objective that you can grow forward most easily in year 1. Check in the column labeled "Year 1."

2. Decide which strategy objectives can be developed best for years 2, 3, and 4. Check in the appropriate columns.

	Year 1	Year 2	Year 3	Year 4
Increase the number of new giving and pledging households.				
Advance the number of people who participate.				
Increase the giving of current giving and pledging households.				
Advance the congregation's giving a quantum leap.				

Each year, positively reinforce the strategy objectives that you have well in place.

Strategy Objectives: Specific Objectives for Each Year of Your Long-Range Plan

Our objective is to increase the number of new giving and pledging households by _____ percent in year ___.

There are four principal groups with which you could advance the number of new giving and pledging households.

Identify the number of households in each group. Then select the specific groups with which you plan to focus your giving campaign.

members who have joined during the current year _____

members who have joined during the past three years _____

worship participants _____

active constituents _____

Our objective is to advance the number of people who participate by _____ percent in year ___.

Specifically, we plan to advance the number of people who participate in each of theses areas by

planning the mission for the coming year _____

developing the mission budget for the coming year _____

participating in the giving campaign _____

Our objective is to help _____ percent of our current giving households to increase their giving in major ways in year _____.

There are three principal groups with which you could advance the number of new giving and pledging households.

Identify the number of households in each group. Then select the specific groups with which you plan to focus your giving campaign.

people whose giving has remained the same for
two or more years   ___

people who have decreased their giving during the
current year   ___

people who have given in prior years and have not
given in the current year   ___

Our objective is to advance the congregation's giving a quantum leap of _____ percent in year _____.

There are four principal groups most likely to help with the congregation's quantum leap in giving.

Identify the number of households in each group. Then select the specific groups with which you plan to focus your giving campaign.

major mission priorities   ___

shepherding   ___

active participation   ___

significant relational groupings   ___

Chapter 6

Campaign Organizations

Structure follows strategy. Form follows function. Organization follows objectives.

You now have well in place:

- the five steps of a giving campaign
- your strategy objectives for the coming four years

From your study of *Giving and Stewardship in Effective Churches* you also will have developed

- the principles for giving
- the six sources for giving
- the motivational resources for giving
- positive reinforcement
- an understanding of stewardship

Now, organize the structure for your giving campaign in a way that advances the giving of your congregation.

Giving campaigns are organized usually in one of these four ways:

- by significant relational groupings
- by congregation
- hierarchically
- geographically

Each of these organizational structures has advantages and drawbacks. You will want to weigh in your mind which of these structures will be of most value to your congregation as you seek to grow forward the generosity of people's giving.

The first way of organizing your giving campaigns is around the significant relational groupings within your congregation. A significant relational group is:

> any group that delivers to the people within it significant relationships of roots, place, and belonging, a sense of sharing and caring, a spirit of family and friends.

Significant relational groupings may include formalized groups such as the Sunday school classes, the adult choir, the women's group, and so on.

Significant relational groupings can be informal as well. These informal networks of relationships are most important. On a Sunday morning, before or after church, you will see people standing around and sharing with one another. They are showing you the informal significant relational groupings of which they are a part. Whenever there is a tragedy or a crisis within a given family, these informal groupings are quick to respond in helpful ways. To be sure, the more formalized groups usually also respond, and frequently the informal and formal groupings overlap with one another.

We live primarily in significant *relational* grouping "neighborhoods." The relational neighborhood is first in value and importance in peoples' lives. We also live in:

vocational neighborhoods

sociological neighborhoods

geographical neighborhoods

genealogical neighborhoods

The best way to organize your giving campaign of "who will contact who" is through the significant relational grouping neighborhoods within your congregation. There are several advantages to organizing your campaign this way. First, this campaign organizational structure embodies the giving principle that "people give money to people." It is through the communication grapevine and networking of the significant relational group that people best know:

- who their giving will be helping

- who will be doing the helping

- who has made the decisions for our mission during the coming year

The most significant networks of communications are within these significant relational grouping neighborhoods.

Second, this structure supports the giving principle that "who asks who is decisive." It may be through:

- the small-group gatherings or dinners, where the host and hostess are a part of a specific significant relational neighborhood

- an every-member canvass in which people call on and contact people within their own significant relational grouping

- telephone contacts within the significant relational grouping

Again and again, whatever the methodology, you are honoring the close networking of relationships—the roots, place, and belonging—that are decisive in people's lives.

It is better to invite people to drive their car five minutes farther across the community to call on someone within their significant relational grouping—even if the call involves simply handing them the mission budget and their invitation giving card—rather than asking them to go five blocks within their geographic community to call on someone they may not know well and who is not a part of their significant relational grouping.

People have already organized themselves into these significant relational groupings. Organizing the campaign in this way has the additional advantage that it is the natural way to organize. You are patterning your campaign structure along the relational lines that are already in existence. You don't have to reorganize your congregation into some unfamiliar structure. They live their day-to-day lives in this relational structure. It is natural for them.

The primary drawback to this approach is that the leadership team will need to take a little time to puzzle through who really relates with whom in which significant relational grouping.

Overall, organizing by significant relational groupings is the most effective and successful campaign structure for your giving campaign. Rural congregations have understood this for years. It may take some time the first year to puzzle through who is in which significant relational grouping. From then on, year after year, the campaign structure is in place, and it is a matter of making appropriate adjustments as life moves forward.

The second way of organizing your giving campaigns is congregationally. Essentially, this approach divides the congregation into several *equal* divisions, usually three or four. As best one can do it, each division has the *same number of households* and the *same total giving* during the current year.

This is a grassroots congregational approach in which the leaders, team captains, and workers within each of the divisions have virtually equal opportunities—with the same number of households and the same total giving record—to grow the giving of the congregation forward.

There are balance and equity in the divisions of the campaign. Each division gets approximately equal representation of:

- major gifts families

- families who increased their pledge during the current year

- families whose pledge has remained the same for two or more years

- families who decreased their pledge from the previous year

- families who canceled their pledge for the current year

- potential giving and pledging households who have no pledge or giving record in recent years

Every effort is made to ensure that each division of the campaign has an equal opportunity to grow forward the giving among the households with whom they are making contact.

For example, a congregation with four hundred households would have approximately a hundred households in each division. The major gifts households would be distributed throughout the four divisions as evenly as possible, as would members of the other five categories above. Each division would get approximately the same number of potential giving households who are not now pledging.

A major advantage of the congregational campaign structure is the genuine sense that all the workers and leaders in the campaign are starting out on an equal footing, with the same opportunity as that of other divisions to grow forward the giving of the households within their division. This approach to campaign structure encourages a stronger sense of ownership among the workers and leaders. It mobilizes their best creativity as they make the invitation contacts with the people who are being asked to give.

Also, this congregational approach communicates to the congregation that this is a grassroots congregation, a grassroots campaign structure, and a grassroots effort to raise giving on behalf of the mission. This campaign structure teaches grassroots members that their giving counts in equal measure with the major givers of the congregation. It develops a spirit of community.

Third, there is a genuine sense in which the premium value and focus of this campaign structure are to help people who are not now giving to come on board with their giving and their pledge. It helps the congregation to grow forward the giving among potential giving households.

The drawback to the congregational campaign structure is that it takes some thought and planning to ensure that the divisions are reasonably balanced. At the same time, this is one of the two most effective campaign organization structures, the other being the significant relational group structure.

Some congregations have successfully combined the significant relational group campaign structure and the congregational campaign structure. They have helped the four equal divisions to be organized around the significant relational groups. That usually means that certain adult classes participate within certain divisions. An effort is made to create some balance as these significant relational groups are placed in each of the four divisions. As much as possible, the same number of households, the same total giving, and the same number of potential giving households are in each division.

One way to bridge from the one structure to the combination would be to organize your campaign along the lines of significant relational groupings for three years. In the fourth year, include the congregational structure and combine it with your previous relational structure.

The third way of organizing giving campaigns is hierarchically. In this hierarchical campaign structure there are also generally four or more divisions:

- a major gifts division, consisting of the significantly higher-giving households
- an advanced gifts division, consisting of higher-giving households
- a special gifts division, consisting of those households whose giving is above average
- a general gifts division, consisting of everybody else (those whose giving is average and below)

The potential giving households are usually placed in the general gifts division.

The major gifts division is typically worked first, and the announcement is made of what these few people are doing in major ways to help the congregation. The advanced gifts division is worked next. The hope is that the major gifts division will set the pace; their precedent will help grow forward the gifts of the advanced gifts division. The special gifts division is worked third with the hope that, by now, most of what is needed to meet the budget has been raised. The general gifts division is worked last with the hope that the balance yet needed will come from within the grassroots of the congregation.

This approach reinforces the value and importance of the higher-giving households who are currently giving a large portion of the money.

Sometimes the message is:

> Were it not for these faithful few who are giving most of the funds in this congregation, this congregation would be in serious financial trouble.

This approach does not share a message that communicates a theology of community.

Some campaign organizers like the hierarchical campaign structure mainly because it is a simple way to raise money. They can get in quickly, raise most of the money from a small number of households, and have a "successful" campaign.

This campaign structure also appeals to some pastors and finance committees because it enables them to contact the fewest number of people, raise the greatest amount of money, and breathe a sigh of relief that the campaign is over and also "successful"—the budget has been raised.

The hierarchical approach to giving campaigns has several difficulties. Yes, it is simple and quick. Yes, it gets it over with. And yes, the money is mostly raised among a few people. However, if you look at its effects over a several-year period, you will see that it can have damaging consequences for the congregation. This hierarchical approach does not:

- help the grassroots advance in their giving
- grow the grassroots forward in their participation in God's mission
- develop a theology of community

These are the primary drawbacks of the hierarchical approach. It misses many in the grassroots—the biggest portion of the households in the congregation. To be sure, they receive the mailings. They are invited to the meetings. They are preached to on the Loyalty Sundays. They are sent pledge cards and asked to bring those cards in with their pledge. They are visited. But they get nowhere near the same personal attention as is given to the current higher-giving households. Thus, life goes on much as it has been. The same few people give most of the money year after year after year. This hierarchical approach does not inspire giving among the grassroots.

More often than not, there are many potential major gifts among the grassroots. These gifts are never realized because of the focus on current major givers. Further, the many potentially generous gifts of grassroots people are lost year after year.

Also, a not-too-subtle message is delivered that this is a "big-money" church, that the grassroots do not count as much—they are not as "important"—as the top givers. That message frequently creates passive-aggressive behavior, low-grade hostility, subliminal resentment, eruptive forms of anger, and low morale among the grassroots.

This approach sometimes communicates the message to the grassroots that their giving is not needed. That message quickly translates into "if my giving is not needed, then my participation may not be needed." The hierarchical approach diminishes the possibility of people's participation in God's mission. It concentrates too much on the favored few.

Finally, the hierarchical approach erodes a theology of community. It creates a priesthood of major givers, not a priesthood of all believers. Some pastors and key leaders speak of "participatory leadership," but then they construct an antithetical approach in their giving campaigns. This incongruity is crystal clear to the grassroots.

Live out in your giving campaigns your theology of community. Look to the future. The more people who discover that their giving counts, the more people who know that they count in their mission.

The fourth way of organizing a giving campaign's structure is the geographical approach. It is based on one principle—people are asked to contact other people who live in their same geographical area. However, the least influential neighborhood in which people live is the geographical neighborhood.

Many years ago, that was not the case. People who lived up and down a given road lived in the same relational and vocational neighborhoods, the same sociological and genealogical neighborhoods—and they also happened to live in the same geographical neighborhood.

During past years, many congregations made efforts to organize themselves into geographical groups. It worked better years ago than it does today, but the reason it worked in those days had very little to do with the geography itself. It was simply that in those days many of the geographical neighborhoods had an overlay of the relational, vocational, sociological, and genealogical neighborhoods. It worked fifty years ago because of those factors more than because of geographical proximity.

The geographical approach is the least effective of the giving campaign structures. Yet people are drawn to it—and this is its primary advantage—because the people organizing the campaign can do it easily. They do not have to think of who relates to which significant relational grouping; they do not have to think of how to create four reasonably equal congregational divisions. They simply take the addresses of who lives where and organize the campaign that way.

Campaign organizers often justify using this geographical structure by saying either (1) "we are saving the workers time—they don't have to travel far from home" or (2) "this would be a good way for people to meet their neighbors who are members of this congregation." As a matter of fact, *neither* of those reasons has anything much to do with effective giving development.

"Who asks who for the money" is decisive, no matter how far they have traveled to make the call. If you would like people to get to know one another, choose some other time during the year and have geographical neighborhood get-togethers. Don't tie it to your giving campaign. When you are trying to grow forward the generosity of peoples' giving, keep focused on that objective.

Structure follows strategy. Develop the structures that advance people's giving. In the long term, the significant relational groupings and the congregational campaign organizations advance giving development. These structures will grow best the generosity of your congregation.

Chapter 7

Selecting Fund-Raisers

Many congregations grow forward their own giving with constructive giving campaigns. They develop solid strategy objectives. They create strong campaign organizations. They advance the principles, possibilities, and motivational resources for giving. They share positive reinforcement. They build an understanding of stewardship. They do it well themselves.

Many other congregations benefit from the assistance of a fund-raiser. Over the years I have had the privilege of working with many excellent fund-raisers who have done solid work.

As you consider working with a fund-raiser, I recommend that you consider working with the same fund-raiser for four years in a row. Develop, in consultation with your fund-raiser, your long-range plan of strategy objectives for the coming four years. Accomplish this strategic planning well. It will help your fund-raiser's work to have lasting value.

This four-year relationship will grow the giving of your congregation in strong, solid ways. Some churches employ a fund-raiser for one year. Frequently, they are looking for a quick fix—and they may achieve it. Yet what helps most is growing the generosity of your congregation over the long term. This will help God's mission best.

Four factors will help you decide when you can benefit best by bringing in a fund-raiser.

The first factor is resources. An excellent fund-raiser will be a major resource to your congregation in these areas:

- the five steps of a giving campaign
- strategy objectives
- significant relational grouping and congregational campaign organizations
- mission planning budgets
- the principles for giving
- the six sources of giving
- a theology of stewardship that is biblical and focuses on the stewardship of God's mission

A primary resource that excellent fund-raisers bring is their consultation. They bring wisdom and experience. You have an on-site person serving as your giving development consultant. You are not simply purchasing a package of materials from some organization. You will be helped better by having a giving consultant for four years than a fund-raiser for one year.

Your giving consultant takes the above-listed resources and tailors them to your congregation. This person serves as your consultant on the best ways to grow the giving of your congregation. Together, you develop your four-year giving development plan based on the strategy objectives. Over the four years, you grow the principles for giving. You develop the six sources for giving. You advance the motivational resources for giving. You create positive reinforcement. You build an understanding of stewardship.

Your giving consultant—long-range fund-raiser—will also bring resources that include a range of sample mailings, publicity materials, ways of doing report meetings, ways of organizing congregation-wide gatherings, and so on. These resources are, therefore, now available to your congregation, and together you can tailor them in appropriate ways.

The second factor is time. Competent fund-raisers save time. It is not simply their expertise in fund-raising. The time they devote to the giving campaign is time that other people do not need to give. In a congregation that is actively engaged in mission, a factor to consider is how much time is to be taken away from those endeavors to focus on the giving campaign.

You do want a fund-raiser who understands that, in fact, the mission of the congregation needs to continue to move forward during the campaign, as well as before and after. You are not looking for a fund-raiser who asks the whole congregation to stop everything else it is doing in order to become totally preoccupied with the giving campaign. When a congregation stops everything it is doing to focus on fund-raising, it loses some of the best reasons for people to give.

The mission teams need to continue their work. The shepherding teams need to continue their work. The worship teams need to help us continue to have corporate, dynamic worship. The leaders of groupings and programs need to continue in solid fashion. People need to continue to discover help, hope, and home.

These are the reasons people give. You want a fund-raiser who knows and understands this. You want someone who continues to see the whole, even while helping you with one part. You want someone who will encourage these activities to be at their best during the giving campaign. You are not looking for someone who calls "time out" on everything else. You are looking for someone who saves you time because you need to be about the business of your mission.

The third factor is effectiveness. Excellent fund-raisers are effective in what they do. Giving development happens. Substantive monies are raised. The key word is *excellent*.

You will benefit from an excellent match between a fund-raiser and your congregation. It is important to achieve an excellent match. Wherever there is not such a match, unpleasant experiences occur. People say, "We will never have a fund-raiser again." Give careful attention to who you employ as your fund-raiser.

The effectiveness of an excellent match will do much to grow the strength and vitality of your whole congregation. You will develop the sense of a winning cause. People will discover a spirit of compassion and a sense of community.

The fourth factor is leadership. Does your congregation have leaders with competencies for growing forward the giving—and can these leaders give the time and effort needed without diminishing their work in other congregational areas?

Many congregations have strong leadership resources heavily engaged in mission, visitation, worship, groupings, and program. They may not, for the moment, have the leadership resources in place to grow forward the giving of the congregation. Frequently, therefore, a fund-raiser supplements the leadership resources in the congregation.

You can employ a person with solid competencies in fund-raising just as you employ a choir director to supplement the music resources present in the congregation or a youth director to supplement the resources for youth leadership within the congregation.

You are, in effect, employing a short-term, part-time staff person who brings considerable competencies in the field of giving development. If you already have competent giving development leadership within your congregation, you will not need supplemental help every year.

Invite an excellent fund-raiser to work with your congregation for a four-year period. This will help to grow the leadership for giving development in your congregation. Invite the fund-raiser back to work with you periodically thereafter to assist in developing your own leadership team over the years.

Once you have decided when you want to use a fund-raiser, you are faced with making the big choice—which fund-raiser will work best with your congregation? I encourage you to use an interview process much as you would if you were hiring any staff person. Interview several candidates, not just one. Consider these criteria when interviewing various fund-raisers:

- strategy objectives
- campaign organization
- motivational resources
- positive reinforcement
- person, not firm

- relational, not functional

- goals

The first criterion is strategy objectives. Look for fund-raisers whose pattern is to help congregations create a four-year giving development plan of strategy objectives. Your giving development will have ongoing meaningful direction and lasting value.

Look for fund-raisers who, with a four-year plan of strategy objectives, have helped congregations grow forward their giving by a quantum leap. You are looking for an organization that has a track record of working with congregations over a several-year period with sufficient regularity that they coach—in consulting ways—the giving forward.

The second criterion is campaign organization. Will this fund-raiser organize the campaign in such a way that it will help you to achieve the strategy objectives you are planning to accomplish?

When a fund-raising organization says, "Well, we use a bit of all four; that's what we do anyway," press them more closely. Discover which of the four is, in fact, persistently predominant in the way in which they have done campaigns. It does not help to employ someone who simply agrees, "Well, we'll do a bit of all four," if they then do things their own way without tailoring what they do to your congregation.

An important point: the leadership of the congregation is in the best position to decide which of the four campaign organizations makes best sense to use during a specific giving campaign. The fund-raisers will be working for you. You will not be working for them. You will want *them* to accomplish *your* fund-raising strategy objectives using the campaign organization *you* help select.

The third criterion is motivational resources. When you want to raise money primarily from among the key leaders, a fund-raising organization that focuses on commitment and challenge will do the job well.

When you want to grow forward the giving primarily among the grassroots members, then look for a fund-raising organization that has experience in focusing on the motivational resources of compassion and community. The content of their campaigns lives out a spirit of compassion and a sense of community. These are the motivation resources upon which they build, and, as much as possible, the fundraiser personally has the spirit of compassion and community.

Look for an organization that understands the five motivational resources and will tailor-make its previous campaigns to the motivational resources that will be most helpful with your congregation.

A fourth criterion is positive reinforcement. Look for a fund-raising organization that knows how to deliver positive reinforcement, goodwill, and thank-yous.

You do not want a fund-raising organization that uses tactics of complaining, lamenting, scolding, and whining or that delivers negative reinforcement. They may be able to raise your budget in a quick and dirty way, but they will leave a legacy of negative reinforcement, passive-aggressive behavior, low-grade hostility, subliminal resentment, eruptive forms of anger, and low morale among the grassroots of your congregation. You will find it even more difficult during the next three years to grow forward the giving of the grassroots. You can avoid this by looking for an organization that knows how to share positive reinforcement.

The fifth criterion relates to the person you are hiring. You do not hire the firm, you hire the person. Even if the firm assures you that they will assign "the very best person available at the time," don't hire the firm. Look for the person who:

- matches well with your congregation
- is familiar with the resources of this book
- knows the resources in *Giving and Stewardship in an Effective Church*
- practices the principles in both books
- has had solid success in recent giving development projects in local congregations
- brings wisdom and experience to the task

Interview the actual person who will be assigned. It will not help you to interview the president of the fund-raising organization and then discover that the person assigned to your fund-raising campaign is someone else. The only person the congregation is ever going to see is the individual the firm sends to do your campaign.

Apply the same thoughtful criteria to your interview that you would use if you were interviewing a director of music, a youth director, or an associate pastor. You know the competencies you look for in those positions. Plan for equally thoughtful interviews with the individuals who would represent the firms under consideration for your giving campaigns.

The sixth criterion is relational—"people skills." Look for a person and a firm who are more relational than functional. Sometimes a congregation describes their fund-raiser as someone who came, did the job, raised the money, and left. Mostly, it was a very functional relationship.

Whenever there is an excellent relational match between the person who served as fund-raiser and the congregation, I hear again and again:

> This person came, liked us—fell in love with us. We came
> to know this person. We had a grand time and became
> friends. They did good work. We were sad when it was time
> for them to leave. We look forward to their coming again.

The success of any given campaign is important. The long-term success of your giving development plan is more important. Your long-range plan is more likely to succeed when the fund-raising person and the campaign approach have a person-centered, people-centered, relational focus rather than a functional, institutional, organizational focus.

The seventh criterion relates to goals. Look for more than whether they have achieved the goals in previous congregations with which they have worked. If a fund-raising organization has set goals so low that they can always succeed in raising their goal, they have created a false positive impression. Some fund-raising organizations set three goals: low, middle, and high. If the low goal is low enough that they can easily reach it, they can say that they have always reached their goal.

You want a fund-raising organization that will help grow and stretch your congregation's giving in realistic, achievable ways. It is important for you and the fund-raiser to participate together in deciding the realistic and achievable goal for your congregation's giving campaign. When fund-raisers say that they alone will decide the campaign goal, be cautious. Some organizations frequently understate goals. They always achieve their goal, but much giving is not raised because of the understated goal, and that is money that is lost. Of course, it is unfair to ask a fund-raising organization to try to reach a high goal that has no basis in reality. That is no better than setting a low goal that is too easily attainable.

When a fund-raising organization suggests three goals, generally they hope to achieve the middle one. Look closely to discover whether the middle goal is understated. Or is it a goal that is both realistic and achievable and also stretching?

In considering various fund-raising organizations, search out answers to these questions:

- What has been their track record with comparable projects and commensurate congregations? As best you can, compare apples and apples. A firm that can raise giving in a "big-money" congregation is frequently lost in a "grassroots" congregation in which there are no big gifts. Determine whether their experience is primarily in growing or declining congregations.

- What has been the pledge shrinkage rate? Is the amount raised in pledges realistically close to the amount subsequently given?

- What happened to the giving in the three years following their participation with a given congregation?

Excellent fund-raisers do solid work. These criteria will guide you in selecting one that will be an excellent match with your congregation. When you find one who knows the principles for giving, the possibilities for giving, and the motivations for giving, develop an excellent long-term relationship with them. The generosity of your congregation will advance to help the mission even more.

Evaluation of Possible Fund-Raisers for Our Congregation

Evaluation Criterion	Possible Points	A	B	C
1. Strategy objectives for the coming four years	15	___	___	___
2. A campaign organization that builds on groupings and is congregational	10	___	___	___
3. The motivational resources of compassion and community	20	___	___	___
4. A spirit of positive reinforcement, goodwill, and thank-yous	15	___	___	___
5. The person you are hiring: is an excellent match with your congregation is familiar with this book and *Giving and Stewardship* practices the principles in both books has been solidly successful in recent projects brings wisdom and experience	20	___	___	___
6. Relational competencies stronger than functional competencies	10	___	___	___
7. Realistic and achievable goals that stretch us to increase our giving	10	___	___	___
Total score	100	___	___	___

PART THREE

Setting Giving Goals

Chapter 8

Giving Patterns Fluctuate

The third area of effective church finances is setting giving goals. Goals are the wings of vision. Goals give life to the vision. What raises the giving is the vision. The stronger the vision, the more generous people are.

Build goals reaching toward your vision. People work toward solid goals. The life of the vision is giving goals. The generosity of your congregation will grow. The best goals:

- have strong grassroots ownership
- are specific and measurable
- are realistic and achievable
- have solid time horizons
- complement each other
- grow the congregation forward

Giving goals that meet these criteria advance the confidence and trust of the congregation. Resist having no goals. Refrain from exaggerated or generalized goals.

Vision involves confidence and trust. Exaggeration does not help confidence. Inflated goals do not help trust. People achieve goals in which they have confidence and trust.

Build giving goals based on:

- your giving pattern
- projecting your budget
- new developments

You will have goals that help grow the generosity of your congregation. You can set giving goals for three time frames:

- immediate, which focus on monthly giving goals for the current year
- midrange, which focus on giving goals for the end of the current year and the end of the coming year
- long-term, which focus on giving goals for years 3 and 4 of your giving development plan

All three giving goal time frames help. You are in the strongest position to set immediate goals for each month of the current year.

Select your giving goal for each month based first on your congregation's giving pattern. This monthly giving goal helps the finance committee to know whether the congregation is "on target" each month in its giving. The finance committee has an indicator of whether the congregation's giving is running ahead or falling behind.

Select your giving goal for each month, based on an accurate analysis of your giving pattern. Then you will be in the best leadership position to encourage the giving of your congregation. Give up using one-twelfth of the budget as a monthly goal. It is inaccurate. Giving patterns fluctuate.

In many congregations in the northern hemisphere, the giving during January, February, and March starts out pretty consistently, with occasional fluctuations caused by adverse winter weather. April shows an increase in giving, based on increases in worship attendance on Palm Sunday and Easter. May drops off. June drops off a little more as attendance also drops with summer school holidays. July is oblivion.

August starts back. September shows another increase, with programs and activities starting up again. In many congregations October shows a significant dip. In some congregations it is the second- or third-lowest giving month of the year.

People are catching up on back-to-school and vacation expenses showing up on their credit-card statements at the end of September and in early October. Then, November does better. In many congregations we "head to glory" in December.

The giving pattern frequently looks like the one shown in Figure 1.

In some congregations, the giving goal for each month is published in the newsletter or bulletin. An excellent way to do this is:

- Our giving goal for *March* was _____.

- Contributions given in *March* were _____.

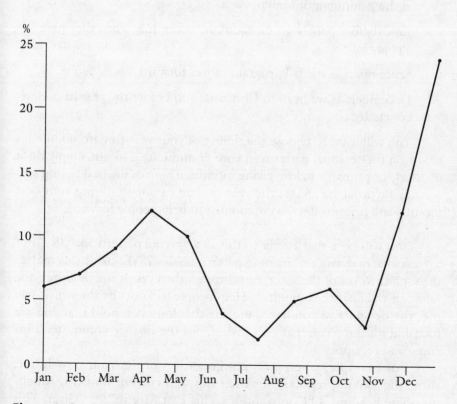

Figure 1: Common Giving Pattern Fluctuations

You may want to add the giving goal for the coming month as well:

- Our giving goal for April is _____.

- Contributions so far in April are _____.

From time to time, you may want to also share a year-to-date summary:

- Our giving goal for January through March was _____.

- Contributions given January through March were _____.

Usually, the year-to-date summary of the congregation's giving is best shared at the beginning of:

April: as we head to Easter. When Easter is earlier, share the report at the beginning of March.

June: before people go on vacation, not in July when they have already left.

September: as the fall program moves forward.

December: as we head to Christmas and before the year has concluded.

You will want to choose the timing of your year-to-date summaries based on the seasonal patterns in your community. Do not simply do it quarterly or primarily in low-giving months. Think of the best timing seasonally. Be proactive. Share the year-to-date summary during your best months and prior to low-giving months to help people forward.

You will note that I refer to this as a "*giving* pattern analysis," not a "receipts analysis" or "income pattern analysis." Look at this matter through the eyes of the giver, not through the eyes of the treasurer, the teller, or the finance committee. Help people to know by the words you use, the perspective you have, and the theology you hold that you are focusing on the congregation's giving, not the finance committee's income and receipts.

For example, when your congregation prints your newsletter, show the "giving reports" for the prior and current months. An appropriate heading is "Contributions This Past Month" or "Given This

Past Month." Do not use words like "Received" or "Receipts This Past Month."

Be certain to look at this through the eyes of the givers. Say "our giving goal" or "our contributions goal." Do not say "receipts needed this month" or "income needed this month." Through the eyes of the givers, these monies are gifts and contributions, not receipts or income.

If your congregation has income from rental properties, investments, or whatever, share that information separately. Do not merge contributions and other sources of income into "receipts needed this month." Doing so would be mixing apples and oranges. Sharing "our giving goal" better encourages giving.

Many congregations' giving pattern is like the one illustrated in Figure 1. If they use one-twelfth (1/12) of the annual budget as their monthly giving goal, the first eleven months of the year they would be falling short of 1/12 of the budget. To expect 1/12 each month for them is unrealistic, and the monthly report of giving would give an unnecessarily negative report for eleven of the twelve months!

There was a time when I referred to the 1/12 basis of analysis as "the old method" and the giving pattern analysis as "the new method." But I discovered in my research that the 1/12 approach is a comparatively recent method of analysis in the life of local congregations. In a barter economy, the 1/12 method was never used. Everyone knew that the major giving occurred at the time of the harvest. The older methods— often informally and intuitively—thought through the giving patterns.

The 1/12 method is a comparatively recent phenomenon. The 1/52 basis of analysis is simply the 1/12 method adjusted to week-by-week use. If you could give up something for Lent during this coming year, give up the 1/12 or the 1/52 method. It is an unhelpful financial analysis. It does not lead to effective church finances. It definitely does not help giving. Fortunately, many congregations have already abandoned this method of assessing whether they are ahead or behind.

In my consultations with local churches, sometimes the leaders will say to me, "Dr. Callahan, we are in grave financial difficulty." Then we sit down and look at the figures. What I discover is predictable—they are using 1/12 of the budget as their monthly giving goals in analyzing whether they are ahead or behind.

These people have not thought through their congregation's giving pattern. What they really have is a cash-flow problem, not a financial problem. Mostly, they are right on track in relation to their giving pattern for the prior three years.

Three things are wrong with the 1/12 method. First, it is inaccurate. As an example of the effect of this inaccuracy, consider a congregation with an annual giving goal of $100,000. The leaders take this total amount of their annual giving goal and divide it by twelve. The result (8.33 percent of the total, or $8,333) becomes their giving goal for each month. However, a giving pattern analysis for their congregation would have revealed that a more accurate giving goal for January would be 6 percent, or $6,000.

Their finance committee announces that the amount needed each month is $8,333. However, in the February board meeting, someone stands and says:

> In January we needed $8,333.
> We only received $6,000.
> We are already behind $2,333.
> Woe is us.

In more than thirty-one years as a consultant, I have never found a single congregation whose giving pattern is equally proportioned, 1/12 each month, over a three-year period. It is inaccurate to use a method of analysis that has no basis in reality. It produces an inaccurate assessment of whether we are ahead or behind in our giving. It has no basis in fact.

The second thing wrong with the 1/12 method is that it is unrealistic. One of the basic principles of giving is:

> People give to their congregation in direct relation to the
> ways in which they receive and expend their income.

They cannot do it any other way. Many people do not receive their income in equal amounts each month. It is unrealistic to expect them to give in a pattern different from the ways they receive and expend their income.

As you stop and consider, you will discover that a substantial percentage of your congregation does not receive their income in equal amounts each month. Farmers don't. Ditch diggers don't. Construction workers don't. Textile workers don't. Waiters and waitresses don't. Salespeople, doctors, lawyers, accountants—all these do not typically receive their income in equal monthly amounts. People in a wide variety of vocations experience fluctuations in income from month to month during any given year.

Yet there are usually just enough people on the finance committee who do receive their income in equal amounts each month, and there is a pastor who would like to receive his or her income in equal amounts each month. Somehow they deduce that therefore the church should receive its income in equal amounts each month. It won't happen. It is simply unrealistic.

I would rather encourage people to give generously as the Lord prospers. This is the biblical principle. You will discover that a wide range of people who practice tithing give differing amounts each month because their income differs from one month to the next.

Encouraging people to practice "regular giving" is helpful. But "regular giving" is not giving the same amount each week or each month. Giving can be "regular" in frequency and yet not in equal amounts each time.

Using 1/12 of the annual goal to assess monthly giving is an unrealistic approach. By using a giving pattern analysis, you respect the fluctuating ways in which people receive their income.

The third thing wrong with the 1/12 method is that it delivers negative reinforcement. In the earlier example, the 1/12 method indicated that the congregation needed $8,333 in January. The giving pattern analysis, based on giving during the prior three Januaries, showed it would be realistic to anticipate 6 percent, or $6,000.

What happens in that congregation when they generously contribute $6,500 in the month of January? Based on the 1/12 method of analysis, someone will stand at the February board meeting and say:

> In January our goal was $8,333.
> We have only received $6,500.
> We are already behind $1,833.
> Woe is us.

I call this "artificial" negative reinforcement because there is no basis in reality for saying they are behind.

Contrast this with the reality that is achieved by using the giving pattern analysis. Then someone could give positive reinforcement by saying:

> Our January giving goal was $6,000.
> The giving during the month was $6,500.
> Thank you for the generosity of your giving to our congregation's mission.

An important point to note here: people do not quit giving when we get ahead on our giving goal, but people do hold back in their giving when someone else takes credit for what they are doing.

For example, if the chair of the finance committee were to stand during the first week of February and say:

> The finance committee's income goal for the month of January was $6,000.
>
> We are happy to announce tonight that the finance committee has successfully raised $6,500 in January alone.

That would be like a coach saying to the team in the locker room after a well-won game:

> Team, I am happy to announce as coach that tonight I won the game.

Imagine how motivated that team is going to be playing next week's game! People do back off on their giving when someone else takes credit for what they are generously giving.

I would rather hear the chair of the finance committee say:

> Our giving goal for the month of January was $6,000.
> This is a very caring congregation.
> We thank you for generously giving $6,500 during January.
> Thank you very much.

The team will play better next week—the generosity of the congregation will grow forward.

There are disastrous results from creating the mentality that the congregation is always behind.

Virtually all congregations know more than 1/12 of their giving occurs in December. In some congregations, the December giving will be 10 percent, 15 percent, or even 25 percent of the year's total giving.

Those congregations that use the 1/12 approach have set themselves up for eleven artificial losing seasons, eleven months of failing to meet the 1/12 goal. At the end of each month—January, February, March, April, May, June, July, August, September, October, and November—someone will stand and say:

> Woe is us!
> Our monthly goal was $8,333.
> We have only received $_____.
> We are behind for the _____ month in a row.

This is eleven months of negative reinforcement.

People give money to a winning cause, not a sinking ship. The 1/12 method creates a false illusion that we are a sinking ship. Thus, if you could give up something for Lent this coming year, I invite you to give up the 1/12 approach.

A giving pattern analysis will help your congregation have more accurate, realistic assessments of how the giving compares with past years—and when appropriate, you can deliver positive reinforcement more often. Well done!

Chapter 9

Your Congregation's Giving Pattern

In your giving pattern analysis, focus on the percent of total giving each month. Ask yourself the question:

> On average, what percent of each year's total giving occurs during January? What percent during February?

To find the average for each month, use the last three years' giving. For example, a congregation's total giving three years ago was $85,000; of that, 7 percent was given in January of that year. Their total giving two years ago was $90,000; of that, 5 percent was given in January of that year. One year ago the total giving was $95,000, 6 percent of which was given in January.

During the previous three years, 7 percent, 5 percent, and 6 percent of the total giving occurred during January. This produces a three-year average for January of 6 percent. Do the same calculations for each month, as shown in Table 4.

Based on the giving pattern of the prior three years, we could reasonably count on 6 percent of the total annual giving goal of $100,000—or $6,000—to come in January.

You can use Table 4 to help you discover the real giving pattern of your congregation during the past three years. Look at the giving of the congregation as a whole, not individual family households and their individual giving patterns. Focus on the pattern of giving during the last three years.

	Total Giving	Jan Feb Mar . . . Dec
Three years ago	85,000	7%
Two years ago	90,000	5%
One year ago	95,000	6%
Three-year average		6%
Coming year giving goal	100,000	
Monthly giving goal		6,000

Table 4: Giving Pattern Analysis

Do an analysis for each month, comparing it to the same month in the three previous years. I usually suggest doing a monthly analysis because many people receive and expend their income on a monthly basis. Remember the basic principle: people give to a church in direct relation to the ways in which they receive and expend their income.

It is possible to do a quarterly analysis. Indeed, some congregations that are overly preoccupied with "where they stand on the money" benefit from a quarterly analysis. They need to focus somewhere other than their preoccupation with money. I encourage such congregations to do a monthly report on mission—the people who this month have discovered Christ; the people served in mission this month—and then, in appropriately balanced ways, to report on their giving each quarter.

It is possible to do a weekly analysis, but this creates too much of a preoccupation with income. So many variables affect weekly giving. A weekly analysis results in too much detail. A weekly giving pattern analysis might help for those congregations whose people receive and expend their own personal income on a weekly basis. Usually a monthly analysis works best for most congregations.

The monthly averages for the prior three years provide a reasonable record of your congregation's giving pattern. Some people have tried looking five to ten years back. Those older figures may be interesting, but they aren't particularly relevant in predicting the giving pattern for the coming year. One variable that can skew the giving pattern is a change in pastoral leadership in recent years—the exit year of the former pastor and the entry year of the new pastor may significantly modify the giving pattern you are seeking to discover.

The two purposes for discovering the pattern of giving in your congregation are to:

- project the giving in the coming year
- encourage giving for the mission budget

The purpose is not to track a historical pattern of many years back. The purpose is to have enough data on the giving pattern to be helpful, but not so much data as to create analysis paralysis. Thus, analyzing the prior three years is sufficient.

Compare percent of giving. In most congregations the total giving amount changes from one year to the next. To discover the three-year giving pattern, you would not compare the dollar amount given in one month of a specific year with the dollar amount given in the same month of the prior year. Comparison of dollar amounts does not clearly project the giving pattern for each month of the coming year in the way that the percent of giving comparison does. If you have other income resources in addition to the congregation's giving—rentals, preschool, and so on—keep your analysis focused on giving amounts. Be careful not to confuse other income with giving. Do not take the data for three years of income from all sources and then use that to project the congregation's giving for the coming year.

Compare apples and apples, not apples and oranges. The best way to determine the focus is to ask yourself the question: "Which do I want to encourage and project: giving or total income?" Then focus on that analysis.

Some congregations find it helpful to focus on their giving pattern analysis for the first two years as they seek to develop a more accurate analysis. Later on they also add an analysis of total income.

Make allowances for major variances. As you look three years back, set aside any major plus or minus variances that may have significantly skewed the prior three years. These can affect the accuracy of projecting the monthly giving goals for the coming year.

For example, there may have been a significant special offering one year that was included with the giving for the annual budget, or a large, one-time gift toward the annual budget may have been given. We would consider setting aside such "plus" factors if we do not foresee a similar possibility happening in the coming year.

During the past three years, were there any major interruptions of worship participation that affected the giving? In some instances, a flood, a major winter storm, or a hurricane can significantly interrupt the worship participation patterns, and therefore the giving pattern may be skewed during that year.

One congregation found it necessary to relocate worship services into their smaller fellowship hall for three months while repair work was being done in the sanctuary. That significantly decreased their worship participation, and the contributions during that three-month period were significantly decreased. You would set aside such "minus" variances as well.

Once you have calculated the monthly average for the prior three years and have put aside any major variances, you have a reasonably accurate giving pattern for your congregation. You can now use this information to project the giving goals for each month of the coming year in an accurate, constructive way.

Table 5 shares an example illustrating the months of January, February, March, and December.

	Total Giving	Jan	Feb	Mar	... Dec
Three years ago	85,000	7%	4%	8%	16%
Two years ago	90,000	5%	3%	6%	18%
One year ago	95,000	6%	5%	7%	20%
Three-year average		6%	4%	7%	18%

Table 5: A Giving Pattern Analysis

	Total Giving	Jan	Feb	Mar . . . Dec
Three-year average		6%	4%	7% 18%
Coming year giving goal	100,000			
Monthly giving goals		6,000	4,000	7,000 18,000

Table 6: Projected Giving Goals

Based on this example's averages, it would be reasonable to project monthly giving goals for January, February, March, and December of the coming year on a $100,000 budget, as shown in Table 6.

Two or three people can develop your giving pattern analysis. It takes a modest amount of time to do the research, determine the percentages and averages, and therefore have a reasonable and accurate basis on which to project giving goals for the coming year.

Include advance giving in your analysis. Some congregations have a significant number of people who contribute in the month of December their full pledge for the coming year. If this is true in your congregation, include the appropriate column in your chart, as shown in Table 7.

	Total Giving	Advance Contributions	Jan . . . Dec
Three years ago		3%	
Two years ago		5%	
One year ago		4%	
Three-year average		4%	

Table 7: Advance Contributions Factor

	Total Giving	Advance Contributions	Jan . . . Dec	After Contributions
Three years ago				2%
Two years ago				4%
One year ago				6%
Three-year average				4%

Table 8: After Contributions Factor

Likewise, include after contributions. Some congregations have a significant number of people who are late in contributing their pledge. They contribute a major portion of their giving in January of the new year to complete their pledge of the previous year. Should this be the case in your congregation, then include the appropriate column in your chart, as shown in Table 8.

Congregations benefit greatly by doing a giving pattern analysis. It helps them to more accurately project their giving for the coming year and to more fully encourage the congregation toward realistic giving goals for each month during the coming year.

A realistic analysis develops momentum. An unrealistic analysis creates the false impression that the congregation is always behind. That damages their morale and drags down the momentum. A congregation with low morale gives less.

Positive reinforcement builds confidence. People move toward mission. Using a giving pattern analysis gives more opportunities for positive reinforcement. Negative reinforcement holds back the mission.

An inaccurate monthly giving goal disguises the resources that are, in fact, present in the congregation and creates the illusion that those giving resources are not present. When that happens, the leaders and the pastor cut back on support for the mission of which they are perfectly capable. That harms the advance of God's mission in people's lives and destinies in grievous ways.

Develop your giving pattern analysis. The generosity of your congregation will grow.

Giving Pattern Analysis

	Total Giving	Advance Contributions	J	F	M	A	M	J	J	A	S	O	N	D	After Contributions
Three years ago															
Two years ago															
One year ago															
Three-year average															
Coming year's total giving goal															
Monthly giving goals for the coming year															

Chapter 10

Projecting Your Budget

Many congregations select their monthly giving goal based on their congregational giving pattern. You can further improve and refine your monthly giving goal by also doing a baseline budget projection.

First, decide what constitutes the "rock-bottom investment budget" for each month during the coming year. You are not necessarily trying to discover month-to-month projections for the whole budget. Instead, focus primarily on those line items that are considered essential.

Budgets are interesting. Frequently, a budget's line items can be sorted into these categories or rankings:

A. Old foundational line items. These are basic to the mission of your congregation, and they have a long-standing history.

B. New foundational line items. These are basic to your congregation's mission, and they are new in recent years or this coming year.

C. Advanced line items. These are usually expended above and beyond the rock-bottom mission necessities budget.

D. Hoped-for line items. Some groups put in line items representing their hopes and dreams for the coming year. Generally, it is understood that "if there is enough money, we will try and do these."

E. Slush fund line items. Some groups include an amount of
money that functions as a slush fund. Generally, two rationales
are given for a slush fund:

- to provide funds that would be helpful "if something were to
  come up"

- to provide a hedge against budget cuts by the finance committee or the board

Frequently, in congregations that have had onerous budget cutting practices, the various committees have learned to "pad" their budgets in order to protect themselves against such cuts. This gives them
something they can cut, or "give away," without seriously affecting what
they really plan to do.

Your baseline budget projection focuses solely on those rock-
bottom dollars per month that will keep the mission moving. You
can go through your budget and rank each line item with an A, B,
C, D, or E, depending on its value in the overall budget. Usually, your
baseline budget projection will include the investment line items ranked
as A and B above.

In some years, you might decide that your baseline budget projection will include all group A line items and some group B line items.
Use your best wisdom. Mostly you will be best served by focusing on
those items that are considered essential for a given year.

Invite your leadership teams to project the timing—that is, during
which month(s) they plan to invest (expend) certain line items related
to their rock-bottom mission. It is important that the chair and several
people of each leadership team (task force or committee) participate in
developing the baseline budget projection for their team.

Each leadership team considers its basic mission plan for the coming
year. Each team decides which baseline budget line items are necessary to
accomplish its mission plan. Each team projects the timing for these line
items on the baseline budget projection chart, as shown in Table 9.

Each team estimates as best as it can when and how much it plans to
invest (spend) for its basic budget line items. An example for a church
school is shown in Table 10.

	Investment Line Item	Investment Amount	J F M A M J J A S O N D
1.			
2.			
3.			
4.			

Table 9: Baseline Budget Projection Chart

Investment Line Item	Investment Amount	J	F	M	A	M	J	J	A	S	O	N	D
Sunday school literature	$600		150		150		100		200				
Vacation Bible school	$300							100		200			
Church school rally day	$100										100		

Table 10: Church School Baseline Budget Projection

The various team projections can then be compiled to discover the baseline monthly budget projections for the coming year.

Granted, there probably are two people on the finance committee who could invest an hour and a half together and, by themselves, reasonably accurately develop a baseline budget projection for the coming year. But that misses the point. The broader the base of the leadership teams who project the baseline budget, the deeper and broader the grassroots ownership for achieving the giving goals for each month.

Developing their own baseline budget projections has these important advantages for your leadership teams.

First, projecting the baseline budget helps each leadership team to do advance planning for their mission. They have a clear sense going into the new year of the key objectives and major accomplishments that they plan to achieve during each month of the coming year.

Second, having the leadership teams project the baseline budget communicates—on the congregational grapevine—the value and importance of what your congregation is about in God's mission. The existence of the baseline budget projection on the informal grapevine helps nurture the giving of the congregation as a whole.

Third, projecting the baseline budget in relation to the giving pattern analysis helps the finance committee to be proactive. For example, for a given month, the baseline budget projection may be higher than the projected giving goal. With this advance knowledge, the finance committee is in a position to take advance action—by encouraging more giving for that month, readjusting the baseline budget for that month, or a combination of both.

There will be months when the baseline budget projection will be lower than the giving goal for that month. That is the time when the finance committee can proactively plan to deploy the "surplus" giving that is expected that month. Likewise, the finance committee can proactively deploy advance contributions.

Fourth, your baseline budget projection helps put the focus on the achievements in mission that are happening month by month during the year. It helps to get the focus away from worrying about whether there will be enough money to pay the bills. If you want to worry about something, worry about whether your congregation is being decisively helpful in the lives and destinies of people. That is worth worrying about. The worry worth lying awake at night about is whether we are strongly, intentionally about God's mission.

In developing your baseline budget projections, the focus is on your expands and adds and your regular items for the coming year. You have studied the twelve central characteristics that grow strong, vital congregations. You've decided on certain of those central characteristics to expand during the coming year. Therefore, the line items that will help you to expand certain central characteristics during this coming year are included as part of your rock-bottom baseline budget. Build your future on what you do best.

In a similar way, the line items for those central characteristics that you plan to add as newfound strengths are included in your rock-bottom baseline budget projections. As part of your baseline budget include sufficient funds to successfully accomplish these adds. You'll be adding new central characteristics that overcome a current weakness and shortcoming. That will greatly strengthen the overall mission and outreach of your congregation.

Further, those line items that are both important and urgent should be included as part of your baseline budget projections. Do not include items on the basis that "we've always done it this way"—that is budgeting based on the past. You want a future-based budget.

A future-based budget grows giving. People are not motivated to give to a past-based budget. Congregations give generously to giving goals that advance the mission.

Baseline Budget Projection Chart

Investment Line Item	Investment Amount	J	F	M	A	M	J	J	A	S	O	N	D
1.													
2.													
3.													
4.													
5.													
6.													
7.													

Chapter 11

New Developments

There will be new developments affecting the giving of your congregation in the coming year. Some to consider are:

- your long-range plan
- new sources of giving
- strategy objectives
- the calendar

The first is the impact of the expands and adds of your long-range mission plan for becoming a strong, vital congregation. The central characteristics you are expanding and adding will have direct and indirect impact upon overall participation.

Most new people are initially sought out by the congregation through mission and outreach, visitation and shepherding. It is not the case that most people seek out a church. Mostly, the church seeks out people. Many of these new people then become part of the service of worship. They begin giving. They contribute recorded contributions and offerings. The more new participants in worship, the more the giving grows. Then, after a time, some of these new people decide to become members.

When you consider the impact of your mission plan on your giving, do not think primarily in terms of how many new members you may receive in the coming year. Rather, project the number of new participating households.

Some congregations decide to add a specific, concrete mission objective as a major contribution to a human hurt and hope in the community. The delivery of concrete, effective help by a competent mission team becomes a legend on the community grapevine. People become part of the mission team. People give more generously to a congregation that is self-giving than to a congregation that is self-seeking. A church that gives itself in mission has less worries for money.

A congregation that adds pastoral and lay visitation as a strong central characteristic will experience an impact in giving. It is not accidental that many people say, "The only time the church ever comes to call is when it wants money." In some congregations, there has been a lack of shepherding for so long that just beginning the visitation program shows immediate results in giving. In other congregations, the development of a substantive visitation program will show results more gradually.

A congregation that expands corporate, dynamic worship will experience an increase in worship participation. The more successful your major community Sundays, the more new worship participants you will have. The more dynamic the music, the more participants will be in worship. The more the sermons have the quality of compassion and the character of grace, the more participants will be in worship.

The more new groupings you start, the more new participants you will have. A congregation that starts three significant relational groups during one year will experience an impact on giving beginning in that year and continuing through subsequent years. The more new groupings a church starts, the less worries it has for money. Many people will become part of the new groups that your congregation is launching in the coming year. Their new giving will help.

Some congregations decide to advance their visibility through signage, landscaping, direct mail, and local media. People begin to say, "Oh! Where did that church come from?"

When churches with inadequate parking add more spaces, there is generally a resultant increase in worship attendance. Shortly thereafter, there is an increase in giving.

The second factor to consider is the six sources of giving. These are discussed in depth in *Giving and Stewardship*. I encourage you to consult the fuller discussion in that work. For the moment, let me suggest that those congregations that make available all six sources of giving do better.

You may have developed a thoughtful plan that, in the coming year, will open new sources of giving—I call these "giving doors." The more all six of these giving doors are open, the more generous your congregation will be. People will have a wider range of ways to express the generosity of their giving. Look at the ways in which this new development will live itself out in the coming year.

Whatever plan you have developed, you can begin to project the influence of opening these giving doors. Congregations with all six doors open develop giving resources. Think through the likely new giving that you will receive as you make available these sources of giving.

The third factor in new developments for the coming year is strategy objectives (see Chapter 5). Many congregations find that the strategy objectives on which they focus in one year shape the giving during the following year.

One strategy objective is to grow new giving households. This may not have been a strong focus for a long time in your church. Thoughtful, caring personal contact with potential giving households will substantively advance the giving during the coming year.

One strategy objective is to involve as many people as possible in the decision-making process that creates the mission plan and budget for the coming year. The more grassroots involvement, the higher the probability that the giving from grassroots sources will increase in the coming year.

One strategy objective is to advance the giving of specific households in the congregation in major ways. Another strategy objective is to grow the giving of the congregation a quantum leap during a particular year.

Have a thoughtful, broad-based approach to these strategy objectives. This is a new development that importantly relates to the strategy objectives that you have achieved and those that you are planning to achieve in the coming year.

The fourth factor to consider is a simple one—the calendar. Take this into account as you develop your giving goals for each month of the coming year. Sometimes, the coming year will include fifty-three Sundays. Sometimes Easter will be in March rather than April. On occasion, Christmas Sunday falls in an awkward position with respect to Christmas Eve, holidays, and vacations. Sometimes school holidays mean that many people will be out of the community on Easter Sunday.

Think through the calendar implications for the coming year. When you give it thoughtful consideration, you will be in a strong position to assess the calendar's effects on each month of the coming year.

Part Three has been about selecting your giving goals for each month of the coming year. These goals will help advance the vision and giving. You will set solid goals when you:

- abandon the 1/12 method

- develop a giving pattern analysis

- project your baseline budget

- anticipate new developments

As you complete each of these four steps, you move into a stronger and healthier position to select your giving goals for each month.

Decide to achieve steps 1 and 2 first—namely, abandon the 1/12 method and develop your giving pattern analysis. On that basis you will have solid giving goals for each month during the coming year. Do steps 3 and 4 as appropriate to fine-tune your goals.

I encourage you to take the giving pattern analysis as a guide, not a literal and legalistic percentage figure. Use your best wisdom and judgment, vision, common sense, and prayer.

Deal appropriately with those situations when you are behind and when you are ahead. Mostly, finance committees become preoccupied with the times they are behind. They don't acknowledge when the congregation is ahead.

Focus strongly on those months when your congregation has achieved the giving goals. That is perhaps the most neglected dynamic in congregations. They become gravely concerned about whether they are going to be behind. They fail to notice—because of selective perception—the many months in which they achieved a realistic giving goal.

The art is to say to the congregation, "Well done." Suppose the giving goal for a specific month is $6,000. During the month, the congregation contributed gifts of $6,000. Say, "Well done." Say it strongly and constructively. Do not take it for granted when the goal is achieved. Encourage the spirit of "well done." You will grow forward the confidence and generosity of people's giving.

When you are behind, based on your giving pattern analysis, say so with confidence and assurance. Avoid scolding or scaring. Refrain from legalism and law. With generosity, say:

> Our giving goal for January was $6,000.
>
> You have generously contributed $5,500.
>
> Thank you.
>
> We will appreciate your help with the remaining $500.

Do not hide that you are behind. Thank people for what they have given. With integrity and expectancy, invite people to help with the shortfall. They will.

Immediate giving goals have to do with monthly giving goals. Midrange giving goals have to do with giving goals for the current year and the coming year. Long-range giving goals have to do with the two years beyond the coming year and in some instances with giving goals that look five to ten years ahead. It is important to be honest with the congregation on these goals.

A regrettable practice in some congregations is the exaggerated midrange giving goal. This practice happens all too often. With respect to the coming year, the thinking usually works like this:

> We really need $100,000 to achieve our mission budget
> for the coming year. We have fallen short in prior years.
> Therefore, we will ask for $130,000, hoping that we might
> achieve $100,000.

This approach undercuts the mutual trust, respect, integrity, credibility, and confidence of the congregation in any annual giving goal. It is doomed to failure.

When you set midrange giving goals, set goals that represent your best wisdom as to what is really helpful to advance the mission in the current year and the coming year. Do not set goals that are too high or too low. Set realistic and achievable giving goals.

Do the same for long-range giving goals. While you may not be able to be as exact with these, seek to set these giving goals with your best wisdom. Be generous, without being grandiose. Be wise, without being too cautious.

Congregations that do well in setting monthly giving goals and midrange giving goals also do the best in setting long-range giving goals. Thus, practice well your setting of these primary goals and you will develop the skill of setting long-range giving goals as well.

Develop giving goals for each month—goals that are realistic and achievable, specific and measurable, with solid time horizons. People are not motivated to give to inaccurate, unrealistic, negative reinforcement goals. People give generously to goals that advance the life of the vision.

PART FOUR

Growing Your Giving

Chapter 12

Easier to Raise

Growing your giving is the fourth area that will help your congregation to have effective church finances. *Giving and Stewardship* is a particularly helpful book for a congregation-wide study of growing your giving. People discover the generosity of their giving and the depth of their stewardship as they study the book.

In addition, you will grow the giving of your congregation by:

- nurturing the habit that it is easier to raise the money than it is to cut the budget

- practicing the gift of encouragement

- taking seriously the various practices of giving present in your congregation

- developing enduring gifts

Congregations that practice healthy habits in these areas develop effective church finances. It is easier to raise the money than it is to cut the budget. Sometimes—after all the pledges, estimates of giving, and other resources are assessed—the total projected giving for the coming year falls short of what you count on as your mission budget.

Note the words. I did not say "what you need" or "what you must have." Focus on "what you count on" or "what will be helpful." Those are perspectives of grace. In an environment of grace, people give more generously. Using the term "what we need" or "what we must have" creates an environment of law. People give less generously in that environment.

When the projections suggest the giving is likely to fall short, many congregations respond in these constructive ways:

- prayer plan

- long-range plan

- constructive combination

Some congregations develop a prayer plan and decide, with integrity, to live on faith. It is not a naive, whistling in the dark optimism. It is not grandiosity or foolish wishful thinking. They live in peace. They live in prayer.

Some congregations decide that the power of their long-range plan—the expands and adds they will achieve— will create sufficient momentum and dynamic. They do this realistically and accurately. They anticipate that during the year there will be enough new giving to overcome the projected shortfall. To be sure, they sometimes decide to defer certain investment items, as they see how the year develops.

Many congregations do both. Their spirit is to live in prayer, to trust in God's compassion. They have confidence in the major priorities of their long-range plan. The vision of their mission is clear and strong. Some new giving will come. The shortfall will be overcome.

Other congregations—and I am sometimes amazed at the number—decide automatically to cut the budget. When a shortfall is projected, their immediate reaction is to cut the budget. For them, cutting the budget has become a habit, a ritual, almost part of their liturgical year. In too many congregations, the nearly suicidal steps each year have become:

- develop the budget

- try to raise the budget

- cut the budget

- repeat the process next year

Cutting the budget has become an anxiously dreaded, routine habit.

It is easier to raise the funds needed to overcome most shortfalls than it is to cut the budget. Invest your time in raising the funds rather than in committee meetings to figure out how and where to cut the budget. It usually takes less time to raise the money than to cut the budget.

Your leadership team will be in a proactive, constructive, and creative stance. You will have more fun. You will grow forward the generosity of people's giving.

Among the present households of your congregation, seven groups can potentially help raise the additional funds when the projections appear to fall short. Select the most likely four of the seven to help overcome the shortfall.

Do not automatically turn to the "stack of cards" of your "regular nongivers" who are dyed-in-the-wool inactive and who have not given to the mission of your church for a long time. Instead, consider thoughtfully and prayerfully what can be done to overcome the forecasted shortfall with some of the following groups.

1. People with a current-year pledge who have not yet made a pledge for the coming year. We have not yet heard from them. Ask yourself how many households there are who have pledges in the current year from whom you have not yet heard. What is the total dollar amount of pledges to the current year's budget that these households are giving?

    You may say, "But we sent them letters. We've had Loyalty Sunday. They received a phone call. They haven't turned in their pledge cards."

    Translation: "We've done everything we know how to do, and we still haven't heard from them."

    Response: "Now is the time to become more proactive with this group of people."

    Before you invest a great deal of energy, effort, and committee meetings figuring out how to cut the budget, ask a task force of several people to phone these people to confirm with them the renewal of their current pledge for the coming year. As appropriate, invite them, constructively and positively, to know that we would appreciate their advancing their pledge for the coming year.

2. People whose prior-year pledge, current-year pledge, and coming-year pledge are at the same level. These people, over a three-year period, have kept their giving at the same level. Select some of those people and families, not necessarily all of them. Invite a task force of several people to contact them and say:

We would appreciate your help. Here is our mission budget. Here is where we are. This is the shortfall. Your help will mean much.

People do not increase their giving gradually. They increase their giving in quantum leaps. They do not start out giving twenty dollars a week one year and the next year advance it to twenty-one dollars, the next year advance to twenty-two, and the next year to twenty-three.

Instead, they go along for several years at twenty dollars a week. Then someone thoughtfully and compassionately invites them to advance their giving. When the invitation resonates with them, they advance their giving to twenty-five or thirty dollars a week. In their eyes, thirty dollars a week is a 50 percent increase in their giving.

3. People whose coming year's pledge is considerably less than what they can give. Do not think primarily of major gifts. Rather consider people whose coming-year pledge might be five dollars a week who are capable of contributing twenty or thirty dollars a week.

Given the projected shortfall, given the solid mission budget for the coming year, give these people the chance to advance their giving. You might say:

This is what we are counting on achieving in mission. The congregation as a whole has responded generously. We do have a projected shortfall. Your help will be greatly appreciated.

Simply and constructively share with them an invitation forward.

4. People who are active constituents and who have some recorded contributions. Perhaps they were overlooked because of a focus only on members. People give generously and graciously to all sorts of organizations of which they are not members, of which they are not even active constituents or participants.

    You might very well contact the people and families who, though nonmembers, participate in some program in your church. Invite them to make a significant one-time contribution. Assure them it will greatly help.

5. People who are active constituents and who have no recorded contributions. To be sure, it is easier to reach constituents who have already made recorded contributions.

    These people benefit from and receive the mission of the congregation. By their active participation they have indicated that "were we to have a church home, this would be it." It is reasonable to consider this group. Invite them to make a significant one-time contribution with the assurance that it will greatly help in the coming year.

6. People, whether members, constituents, or in the community, who have participated in sharing or receiving shepherding in recent times. Note that we do the shepherding for the sake of shepherding. We do not do the shepherding for the sake of raising money.

    These people have participated in the shepherding of your congregation. They are aware of your congregation's mission. They have the sense of your congregation's generosity in helping people. Simply and gently help them know what would help. Frequently, they will give generously and graciously.

7. People with a current-year pledge and a prior-year pledge who have said "no" for the coming year. One year, a task force of two people phoned the people who had already said "no" to some worker in the giving campaign, saying:

We would appreciate whatever you can contribute to the congregation's mission. I'm aware you were contacted earlier. I want you to know your help will be greatly appreciated.

One-third of the people contacted said yes. Over the phone, they said, "Put me down for $_____."

I am not suggesting that you automatically contact *all* of the people who have said "no" for the coming year but who had given before. I am not suggesting you hassle and hustle people. Select whichever of those people might possibly, given a second chance, say "yes."

Remember all of the chances Christ gave to Peter and the other disciples—three or more times he gave them chances to change their way of thinking and doing. Consider all of the chances that God has given to each of us. Quietly and compassionately, give some people a second chance.

Consider these seven groups. Select whichever four groups hold promise for you to raise the additional money from. It will be simpler, quicker, and easier than convening the committee meetings to cut the budget. And you will be helping people grow forward their competency in giving.

I have often wondered why some leadership teams, when there is a projected shortfall, quickly move to the behavior pattern and mentality that says, "Let's cut the budget." They could trust in prayer. They could have confidence in the momentum of their long-range plan to bring in new giving. They could raise additional giving. They could achieve a combination of these three. For example, a congregation might seek to raise $100,000 in pledges. They have a solid giving campaign and raise $90,000. They could decide to:

- trust in prayer: $3,000

- have confidence in the momentum of their long-range plan: $3,000

- raise additional giving: $4,000

Or they could decide to:

- trust in prayer: $3,000
- have confidence in the momentum of their long-range plan: $2,000
- raise additional giving: $4,000
- cut the budget: $1,000

They have a combination of three or four ways of moving forward. Instead, some congregations skip directly to cutting the budget. Why?

One reason is prior experience in the church. People lead in direct relation to how they experience being led. As they were "coming up" in the church leadership circles—on the educational team, or the worship team, or the visitation team—they may have experienced the finance committee cutting their budget.

They finally make it to the finance committee, and they face a projected shortfall for the coming year. So they do what was done to them. They do what they have learned to do—cut the budget. It is a learned behavior pattern.

Another reason is because of their experience in business. They may work in a business environment that is reactive rather than proactive, organizational and institutional rather than missional and relational. Their day-to-day work experience contributes to the way in which they behave in their congregation.

They may not be people who participate in cutting expenses in their business—they may be the victims of those cuts. But what they have experienced is what they bring with them to their church: "Well, we don't like to have to do this, but I guess we're going to have to cut the budget."

Another reason some people gravitate to cutting the budget is as an exercise in power. For highly dictatorial leaders, it is the way in which they ensure that their favored projects get funded, and those projects that they favor less are the ones that are cut.

There are people who do not have an interest in some projects or the people who espouse them. They do not like some projects or the people who espouse them. When there is a shortfall of pledges, they make their power felt by trimming away those parts of the budget. You can know with certainty that they are respected, resented, and feared.

Occasionally, some people are drawn to cutting the budget out of anger. They have worked hard and are deeply committed to their church. They have a quietly resentful anger that the grassroots does not support the church as well as they should.

Finally, for some people, cutting the budget is where their current competencies are. It is what they, for this moment, know how to do. As yet they may not have grown forward the giving principles in their own lives. As yet they may not have developed their competencies for raising additional giving. What they have learned how to do is to cut the budget, and so they head toward what they know how to do.

I encourage these people to consider this:

> You learned how to cut the budget. It is a difficult, awk-
> ward, painful experience for everyone involved. You can
> learn a new way. You can learn how to develop a prayer plan
> and count on the momentum of your mission plan. You can
> learn how to raise additional resources in giving.

If you can learn one way, you can learn an even more constructive way.

Many congregations develop a prayer plan and live on faith. Many count on the momentum of their long-range plan. Many congregations raise additional resources for giving.

Sometimes we do all three of these constructive steps, and yet it also becomes important to cut a reasonable budget. There may be times when it is needful to cut the budget.

Having considered all possibilities, should it make best sense to cut the budget, then I encourage you to achieve two objectives.

First, when you cut the budget, involve as many people as possible in the decisions of what is cut. The appropriate leadership team, broadly based, makes the decision as to what percentage of the total budget needs to be cut.

Then, invite the various work areas, committees, and task forces to do their full fair share in cutting the budget. Let them discover the specific line items they can reduce or eliminate completely. Give each of the work areas the freedom to decide what they want to cut. Do not do this for them. Let them decide.

The more people who are involved in the cutting process, the more people who will show up next year to help raise the money. The fewer involved in the cutting process, the more passive-aggressive behavior that will be created among leaders and grassroots. The fewer involved in the cutting process, the fewer who will show up next year to raise the money.

Whenever the finance committee takes upon itself the responsibility to make all the decisions as to what items shall be reduced or cut completely in the total budget, that finance committee will become respected, resented, and feared. However good their intentions, what is finally communicated to the grassroots, key leaders, and pastor of the congregation is:

> When it comes to making the final decisions as to what will stay in the budget, we are the only ones who will make those decisions.

The finance committee may not do this in a mean, ugly, excessive, self-centered way. Most finance committees, who take upon themselves the total decisions, do this quietly and thoughtfully—with decency, integrity, and honor.

At the same time, when they take upon themselves the responsibility to make all the decisions as to what will be reduced and what will be cut completely, they are severely damaging their own ability to grow forward the generosity and the giving in their congregation. A top-down, centralized approach to budget cutting helps congregations to not raise next year's budget.

The wise finance committee gives leadership to helping the various committees find ways in which they can do their full share in bringing the budget into balance, making the necessary reductions and cuts. This creates a grassroots momentum to ensure that we do not have to do this kind of process again.

Second, put well in place the principles for giving. Use the occasion of cutting the budget to also develop your four-year plan of growing the six giving principles in your congregation. With these principles well in place, you will have a long-range sense of direction. This will help ensure that you will not often have to deal with cutting the budget.

With these giving principles well in place, you can enjoy focusing less on cutting budgets and more on helping people grow the generosity of their giving.

People share their giving generously in an environment of raising the giving. People are not motivated to share their generosity in an environment of cutting budgets. Grow the giving of your congregation. Grow the ways you can raise the giving rather than cutting the budget.

Giving Possibilities in a Projected Shortfall

Identify the number of households in each group.

Select the four of the seven groups with which you can best grow forward the giving.

	Households	Giving Goal
1. Current-year pledge, no pledge for the coming year as yet received.	_____	_____
2. Prior-year pledge, current-year pledge, and coming-year pledge are at the same level.	_____	_____
3. Coming year's pledge considerably less than what they can give.	_____	_____
4. Active constituents with recorded contributions.	_____	_____
5. Active constituents with no recorded contributions.	_____	_____
6. People shepherded recently, whether members, constituents, or in the community.	_____	_____
7. Current-year pledge, prior-year pledge, and "no" for the coming year.	_____	_____

Ways Forward with a Projected Shortfall

Our giving goal is $ _____

Our pledges are $ _____

Our projected shortfall is $ _____

We have decided to

    trust in prayer $ _____

    have confidence in the $ _____
    momentum of our long-
    range plan

    raise additional giving $ _____

Or we have decided to

    trust in prayer $ _____

    have confidence in the $ _____
    momentum of our long-
    range plan

    raise additional giving $ _____

    cut the budget $ _____

Chapter 13

The Gift of Encouragement

Congregations who grow their giving practice the gift of encouragement. They share positive reinforcement. They say "thank you" for people's giving. They discover as many ways as possible to share the habit of saying "thank you." They grow forward the goodwill of the congregation. They create a climate of encouragement.

The thank-you letter, personal phone call, or personal visit can be shared with people—whatever their form of giving. This is one of the simple ways in which you can share the gift of encouragement.

Send people a "confirmation thank-you" immediately upon receiving their pledge. Don't wait. In some churches, the giving campaign is in September, October, or November. The campaign leaders frequently become so busy with the campaign that no thank-you is sent. Indeed, often the only confirmation of their pledge people receive is when they receive their new monthly statement the first week of February or their new quarterly statement the first week of April. This is a poor way to say "thank you."

You can grow forward the success of your giving campaign as you have one or two people send thank-you confirmations the day after each pledge is received. See that a thank-you note is sent that does two things:

- thanks people for their pledge
- confirms their pledge

Make it as personal a note as possible. You will be amazed at what happens on the community grapevine. Those people in the congregation who have yet to make their pledge will be encouraged as those who have receive a genuine sense of personal thank-you, goodwill, and positive reinforcement.

Send a special thank-you to those people and families who have pledged to increase their giving. It will be distinct from the regular thank-you letter for those people who kept their pledge the same. It will be a special confirmation letter for those people who have increased their pledge. It could say something like:

> We very much appreciate your increased giving for the mission of the congregation during the coming year.

Then go on to confirm their pledge.

You honor, thank, and appreciate the fact that they have increased their giving. They are more likely to consider increasing their giving again at some future time because you have shared a thoughtful thank-you for the increase they are now giving. Whenever you take the increase for granted, it is more likely the person will stay on that plateau longer.

Send a special thank-you to people who are making a pledge for the first time. They may have been members of your congregation for a number of years. They may have occasionally given recorded contributions. They may have joined within recent years, but for whatever reason, this is their first pledge.

> We very much appreciate your decision to pledge to the mission of the congregation. It is most helpful. Thank you.

These people live in relational neighborhoods with other people who may not yet have made a pledge. The special honoring of their pledge is an important form of positive reinforcement; it will be a good message on the community grapevine.

Thank new members who have joined your congregation this year for their pledge. When they begin giving, send them a thank-you. Help new members know that their giving means much to the mission of the congregation. It is particularly important with any of these letters that they be sent as soon as possible after you receive the pledge.

Send thank-you statements of contribution. Look at your statements of contribution through the eyes of the giver. Help the statements to be a thank-you note of appreciation. The "thank-you" is on the statements for those people who are giving.

Do not do what one church was doing. They were sending statements of contributions to people who had given nothing and saying "thank you" on those statements. This was their inverted legalistic way of trying to grow guilt so that those people would end up doing something. That approach does not help. Share a positive word of appreciation for what people are giving. In many churches I've suggested to the financial secretary that when they send out the statements to the people who are current in their giving, they should write two words on the statement:

Thank you.

In one church, the financial secretary asked me, "Dr. Callahan, do you really think that will help?" I said, "Yes. Try it. See what happens." I was there a year later for a follow-up consultation. She said to me, with amazement:

Dr. Callahan, I began doing what you suggested, and do you know what happened? People began to write me back thank-you notes, thanking me for thanking them.

It had been years in that congregation since anyone had said "thank you" for people's giving.

Send a thank-you to those people who have recorded contributions. Even if your church does have pledging, there will be people who do not pledge but make recorded contributions. Send them a thank-you. Each time they make a recorded contribution, send them a thank-you. Beyond their recorded contributions, they may decide to become pledging households. The more positively they experience their giving, the more likely they are to decide to become pledging households.

Share a thank-you note with people who make a special gift. Some churches have the illusion that they want to discourage special gifts because they want all the money to go to the annual operating budget. The book *Giving and Stewardship* shares the "six sources for giving" with which people give to the mission. People will give to the operating budget on a regular basis, and from time to time they will also share special gifts. Thank them. They will share with you more special gifts.

Have the spirit of "thank-you" in your newsletter and bulletin. Give up every temptation to put announcements in the newsletter or bulletin that chide and scold. Find creative and constructive ways of sharing positive reinforcement. Help people to have the sense that they are part of a winning team, not a sinking ship. Do that well in the newsletter and the bulletin.

Send a letter of encouragement prior to low-giving months. Give up the "summer slump letter." Some congregations have sent out the summer slump letter for so many years that it has become a tradition.

The summer slump letter has three paragraphs:

Paragraph 1: "The church has gotten a little bit behind on its bills."

Paragraph 2: "The utility bills were higher than we expected."

Paragraph 3: "Could you please send a little money to help us catch up?"

Now, there are only three things wrong with the summer slump letter; other than that, it is a perfectly good letter.

Paragraph 1, "The church has gotten a little bit behind on its bills," reminds people that they are a little bit behind on their bills. Do you know anybody who's ahead?

Paragraph 2, "The utility bills were higher than we expected," has just reduced the winning cause of Christ to a utility bill.

Paragraph 3, "Could you please send a little money to help us catch up?" regrettably, gets people to do just that—they send you a little money. People live forward or downward to our expectancies of them. If you ask for a little money, that's what you will get—a little money. Regrettably, churches receive just enough money that they think the letter works.

Give up the summer slump letter. It describes your congregation as a sinking ship. It is counterproductive and does not help.

Send your letter of encouragement prior to a low-giving month. Act in a proactive way, and send an encouraging letter, not a lamenting one. Choose words that match best with your congregation and community, and communicate this spirit:

Paragraph 1: "Our church is doing solid work."

Paragraph 2: "The lives and destinies of many people are being helped."

Paragraph 3: "Thank you for the generosity of your giving."

You don't even have to say "send more money." They will. People give money to a winning cause, not a sinking ship.

Share positive encouragement in your reports. At your monthly and quarterly meetings, whoever gives the report can help it to be a coaching one, not a correcting one. Help the report to affirm and encourage, not deliver despair and discouragement. Find solid ways to deliver positive reinforcement through your reports and your meetings.

Have constructive finance committee meetings. Many congregations do. The positive reinforcement grows.

Some congregations have too many finance committee meetings. They do more damage and harm than good. This is particularly true in congregations where the tendency of the finance committee meeting is to focus on negative reinforcement.

If your finance committee is meeting each month, one of the best things you can do is to meet once a quarter or slightly more often than that. You will reduce from twelve to four the number of meetings that share negative reinforcement. You will successfully have set aside several possibilities of negative reinforcement. That will help.

Meet as often as makes sense to have constructive meetings. Avoid a routine of "we're always behind" meetings. Advance a pattern of proactive, creative finance planning. Most finance committees can achieve excellent work, focusing on major priorities, in five to seven solid meetings a year. When the committee meets too often, it gets caught up in 80-percenters and negative reinforcement.

At the end of the year, send a thank-you to the people for their giving during the past year. This may also include the record they will need for tax purposes, but there is too much preoccupation with that record. We provide the record as a service. The primary service you can deliver is the thank-you for their giving.

All twelve of these thank-you possibilities are helpful. Develop an action plan for the coming four years. Put some of them into practice this year. By the end of the four years, have the ones you selected well in place.

Congregations grow their giving as they practice habits of "thank-you," as they share the gift of encouragement.

The Gift of Encouragement: Thank-You

1. Decide which "thank-you" practices are already well in place in your congregation. Check these in the column labeled "Well in Place."
2. Select the "thank-you" practices that you can grow forward most easily in year 1. Check them in the column labeled "Year 1."
3. Decide which "thank-you" practices can be developed best for years 2, 3, and 4. Check them in the appropriate columns.

	Well in Place	Year 1	Year 2	Year 3	Year 4
Confirmation of pledge/giving					
Increased pledge/giving					
First-time pledge/giving					
New members					
Thank-you statements					
Recorded contribution thank-you					
Special gift thank-you					
Newsletter/bulletin					
Encouragement letter					
Reports in meetings					
Finance committee meetings					
Year-end thank-you					

Each year, positively reinforce the "thank-you" practices that you have well in place.

Be in prayer for your congregation. Help your congregation sense well the grace of God.

Chapter 14

Practices of Giving

People give to a church in direct relation to the ways in which they both receive and expend their purchasing power in everyday, ordinary life. They cannot do it any other way. Historically and currently, there are five major ways in which people give, based on the different types of economies in which people have lived and are living:

- barter
- cash
- check
- check–credit card
- automatic transfer

Each of these practices has its appropriate value and functions.

In a barter economy, people receive and expend their purchasing power by bartering—trading and exchanging goods and services. They can't do it any other way. Very frequently, a barter economy is a seasonal economy, based on the time of the harvest.

The traditional barter economy was more prevalent in earlier times. Yet there are many places on the planet—and in this country—where a barter economy is still alive and well.

In churches within a barter economy there is no strong emphasis on weekly giving. For them, the practice is seasonal giving. The giving to the church takes the form of a "Lord's acre." A farmer gives several cows.

Families contribute a portion of their canned goods. People give and contribute in the ways in which they exchange their purchasing power in everyday ordinary life. If most of the people in your congregation live in a barter economy, seasonal or quarterly statements of contributions make good sense.

In many places, over time there was a movement from a barter to a cash economy. People began to receive their income in the form of cash in little brown envelopes at the end of each work week. They began to purchase groceries each week with cash. The concept of "cash and carry" emerged. In a barter economy, any groceries purchased were put on the bill until the time of the harvest.

In the developing cash economy churches began to encourage people to give to their church on a regular weekly basis. In a barter economy, the encouragement had been to "give as the Lord prospers." To be sure, it helps to contribute something each week in the offering, but that "something" was to show that you dedicate your whole life to God. There wasn't a lot to give week by week. It mostly all came in at the time of the harvest. The strong emphasis on weekly giving began to flourish in a weekly cash economy.

It took the development of a cash economy, plus the necessity of documenting people's contributions (thanks to the tax laws), to foster the invention of "offering envelopes." The Christian church moved forward on this planet for virtually 1,900 years without anyone knowing what an offering envelope looked like. In a barter economy, you could not put a Lord's acre or a cow into an offering envelope. What you can put into an offering envelope is cash.

When you think about it, offering envelopes are very similar to the little brown pay envelopes in which people received their cash at the end of each week. They are about the same size. The offering envelope is usually white, not brown; the flap runs the long way, rather than on the short end. In a cash economy weekly giving of the same regular amount was encouraged. To encourage that weekly kind of regular giving and to be able to identify people's contributions, weekly offering envelopes evolved.

In many places, we moved through a transition from a cash to a check economy based on the use of checks or bank drafts. People began to give their contributions to their church by check. This transition is still going on in many places; it has yet to occur in others.

During this transition some church treasurers experienced an identity crisis. They would put an announcement into the church bulletin reading something like this:

> Please be sure to use your own personal weekly envelope
> with your own offering number imprinted on it, so that we
> can accurately record your giving.

This was puzzling, especially to people who were giving by check. They were putting into the offering a check with their name signed and printed on it. Surely someone could tell who had given that contribution.

A significant development of the check economy is that people began to expend their purchasing power more on a bimonthly than a weekly basis. In a cash economy, the insurance agent would drop by to collect the insurance premium once a week on Friday or Saturday when people got paid. As we evolved into a check economy, the insurance premiums tended to be paid every two weeks or once a month in response to a statement mailed to the policyholder. Churches found the practice became more and more bimonthly giving.

It is important to note that the movement to a check economy has not been embraced by a large number of people. It is not simply that people who grew up in a barter or cash economy are clinging reluctantly to the approach they learned while young. Many people in this country receive a portion or all of their income in cash. Many do not have checking accounts. They expend their purchasing power either in cash or, on occasion, through money orders.

Many people now live in a check–credit card economy. They pay for many of their purchases by charging to a credit card. They may write a few checks from week to week, but the greatest dollar volume of their check writing is in response to monthly credit-card statements that come to them at a regular predetermined time each month. In churches, this is reflected in the practice of monthly giving.

Many churches mail monthly offering envelopes to their members. People usually respond well. They do so not primarily because of the offering envelopes. It is because of the monthly reminder to contribute generously to the mission of their congregation.

In churches using weekly envelopes, many people discard three of the four weekly envelopes and use one to send in their monthly contribution. Certainly, they frequently also contribute to the offering plate on Sunday morning. But the primary behavior pattern of a check–credit card economy is of a monthly giving nature, not seasonal or weekly.

Thus, churches that send monthly statements of contributions usually do better than those that send out quarterly statements of contributions. This is especially true when most of the people in the congregation function in a check–credit card economy. They are used to writing checks on a regular monthly basis.

People who have moved into a check–credit card economy tend to think on a monthly basis rather than seasonally or weekly. The statement of contributions that comes each month helps them stay current in their giving.

Some people now live in an automatic transfer economy. Their practice is automatic transfer giving. Remember the basic principle: people give to the church in direct relation to the ways they both receive and expend their purchasing power. Frequently, churches now have arrangements in place so that regular contributions may be made by automatic electronic transfer from the contributor's bank account to the church's bank account.

This development follows the trend of many people receiving their income by automatic electronic transfer into their bank account. Many no longer receive a paycheck at work. The money is automatically deposited in their bank account. Their mortgage payment is automatically drawn from their account. Their car loan payment and their insurance payment are automatically transferred. And their contribution to their local congregation is also automatically transferred to their church's account. This way of receiving and expending one's purchasing power is increasingly common.

This is also true with many retired people. Their pension is automatically deposited into their account. Many of these people grew up pri-

marily in a barter economy. They adjusted to a cash economy. They found
their way through a check and check–credit card economy. Now they
practice an automatic transfer way of giving. It is convenient. In a barter
economy, giving the Lord's acre at the time of the harvest is the timely,
convenient way. In a cash economy, receiving your cash in a pay envelope on Friday and putting some of it in an offering envelope on Sunday
is the serviceable, convenient way to do it. In a check–credit card economy, mailing contributions by check on a monthly basis is the practicable,
convenient way to do it.

There will be those who will say:

> Well, if they were really committed, they would put their
> gifts in the offering plate on Sunday morning rather than
> mailing them in or giving them by automatic transfer.

Those who say this are people for whom it is convenient to put their
own offering in the plate each Sunday. It is inappropriate for some to
sanctify their preferred way of giving as the only way of giving.

People who give by automatic electronic transfer are really committed. They give in the fitting, advantageous way that matches the practice with which they receive and expend their purchasing power in their
everyday ordinary lives.

You will be in a stronger position to advance the generosity of your
congregation's giving as you come to understand the variety of economies
in which people in your congregation live. As a result, you will be in
the best position to develop an understanding of the probable ways in
which they will want to give their contributions to the mission of your
church.

Could you convince people to shift from their customary practice of
expending their purchasing power to using a method that you prefer they
use? Yes, it is possible—with stringent, repetitive indoctrination. But my
suggestion is that you help people to contribute generously and graciously in whatever manner they are receiving and expending their purchasing power in everyday ordinary life.

That means that in a given congregation, those people who practice a cash economy in their everyday life will appropriately use offering
envelopes for their cash offering at the church. This does not, therefore, automatically mean that everyone in the congregation must have

offering envelopes. There is nothing ordained of God that says all giving must occur through offering envelopes. Those people who find them helpful are welcome to use them.

Some people will give on a monthly or seasonal basis. Some people will contribute by automatic transfer. And if someone offers a cow or a Lord's acre to the mission of God, you can find a way to use either in the Lord's work.

When you understand well the practices of giving in your congregation, you are in the strongest position to tailor your giving invitations in ways that help people to give generously. You can honor the wide range of practices with which people can contribute generously to the mission of your congregation. You will be helping your people grow forward the generosity of their giving.

Likewise, these practices of giving can inform the way in which your congregation sends statements of contribution. There are three important purposes for a statement of contributions:

- to thank people for the generosity of their giving

- to give encouragement to people when they are beginning to fall behind what they had indicated they would give

- to account accurately for the giving that has been shared

These three purposes are listed in their order of priority. Thus, the statement itself should look as much like a thank-you note as possible, not like a bill. It should embody the spirit of thankfulness and encouragement. You want just enough accounting so that people know their gifts have been properly recorded. You do not want so much accounting that it gets in the way of the statement being primarily a thank-you note and a word of encouragement.

Match the frequency of the statements with the major practices of giving prevalent in your congregation. Now, it is true that some congregations, mostly smaller ones, have an informal network of communications that helps people to be thanked and strongly encouraged for their giving. Such congregations may not need statements of contributions. It is a matter of best wisdom.

Should you decide statements will be helpful, match their frequency with your congregation's giving practices. When the major pattern of giving is related to a barter economy, then send seasonal or quarterly statements of contributions.

Should the prevalent patterns of giving in your congregation relate to a check, a check–credit card, or an automatic transfer pattern, you will most likely find monthly statements beneficial. People who are accustomed to expending their purchasing power on a monthly basis tend to appreciate a monthly statement. It matches the way they practice the expenditure of their purchasing power in everyday life.

The best way forward is flexibility. Share a monthly statement with many families, a quarterly statement with those for whom that will be most helpful, and an annual statement for those whose giving pattern tends to be a one-time annual gift. Think it through in terms of what will be helpful to the people in your congregation.

Do send a thank-you statement of contributions whenever you receive a gift. This may mean that the person who normally receives a quarterly statement may receive a thank-you statement at the end of a month in which they have contributed a gift, even if it is not yet the end of the calendar quarter. That is fine. You are thanking people for their giving.

Send statements that are "giver friendly." Keep the statement of contributions as simple as possible. Regrettably, statements are most often designed by people with a background in accounting rather than a background in giving development. As a result, the statement looks like a detailed accounting analysis. Look at the statement through the eyes of the giver, not the eyes of the accountant.

Use as few digits as possible. When a person has contributed four distinct twenty-dollar gifts in a month, they will know these have been properly recorded when the statement of contributions thanks them for gifts totaling eighty dollars during that month. If you are doing manually prepared statements, it is sufficient to show eighty dollars as $80. You do not automatically need to show it as $80.00.

Showing a six-digit date (00/00/00) and a twenty-dollar amount for each gift is to put a considerable number of digits on the statement.

That provides more detail than is helpful. Also, the total number of digits frequently convinces people they are giving more than they actually are. All those digits are very impressive!

When you send monthly statements of contributions, it is not helpful to itemize each gift contributed during that month. If you feel it important to do so, or the giver wants you to itemize each contribution, you may show it as $20—rather than showing it as $20.00. The basic point is to show as few digits as possible to keep the statement simple and "giver friendly."

Affirm a person's pledge using the same terminology they used when they made the pledge. If the person said on their pledge card:

> Count on me to contribute $20 a week.

then the wording of the statement of contributions appropriately says:

> Your pledge is $20 a week. During this past month your
> contributions have been $80. Thank you for your giving to
> the mission of the church.

Likewise, if they said, "Count on me for $100 per month," let the statement of contributions show their pledge as one hundred dollars each month. It is important to show the lowest dollar figure for the shortest period of time, being faithful to the way the person made the pledge.

When someone pledges a weekly, monthly, or quarterly amount, do not annualize the pledge amount. If someone pledges twenty dollars a week, do not say:

> Your pledge is $1,040 for the year.

If they pledge one hundred dollars a month, do not say:

> Your pledge is $1,200 for the year.

They did not think of it on an annual basis; they thought of it on a weekly or monthly basis. When you affirm the pledge at twenty dollars per week or at one hundred dollars a month, you honor the practice with which they intended to give it.

If you annualize the pledge, you turn twenty dollars into $1,040; you turn one hundred dollars a month into $1,200. This looks a bit overwhelming. It also teaches them that they have the whole year. If they had any tendencies toward procrastination, you encourage that tendency to procrastinate by annualizing the pledge. You also teach them you are not willing to be faithful to the way in which they made their pledge. When you want to encourage regular giving, do not confuse the issue by bringing up annual amounts. Instead, focus on the frequency with which they have indicated they plan to give. Be faithful to them in honoring their giving practice; they are more likely to be faithful to you in their giving.

Some churches send only quarterly statements because they fear that sending monthly statements would be more expensive in personnel time and postage. When your congregation would benefit from monthly statements, the additional investment in personnel and postage can be weighed against the hidden costs of sending only quarterly statements. When people get behind in their giving, sending a quarterly statement is like closing the barn door after the horse has gotten out. It does little good; it may do harm.

People who have a monthly practice of giving sometimes get behind during the course of the first quarter of the calendar year. By the time they receive their quarterly statement in early April, they are sufficiently far behind that it is difficult for them to go back and make up what they have not yet given. This negative experience teaches them that the next time there is a giving campaign, they will keep their pledge low enough so they can afford to catch up when they invariably get behind. When they receive a monthly statement of contributions during the first week in February, they see they have given generously sixty dollars toward their pledge of one hundred dollars per month, and they are only forty dollars behind. They are more likely at that point to catch up by writing a $140 check (one hundred dollars for the new month and forty dollars to catch up).

Likewise, when they receive a statement the first week in March, that statement will help them stay current on their giving in January and February. Under a quarterly statement system, by the time they receive the first statement in early April, it is almost too late.

There will be some additional investment in postage and personnel time to send monthly statements. Weigh the investment in relation to the hidden costs of pledge shrinkage and loss of giving that occurs with quarterly statements. Many congregations that have changed to monthly statements have found the increase in giving to more than outweigh any additional expense.

Some statements of contribution are worth not sending. They are so accounting-oriented and negatively worded that they do more damage than good. Use the following criteria to assess your statements of contribution:

- The frequency of sending matches with the giving practices in our congregation.

- It is an excellent thank-you note.

- It gives positive encouragement to help people stay current in their giving.

- It accounts accurately for their giving.

- It is simple and giver friendly.

Monthly statements of contribution may not be the best way to go for every situation. Do not arbitrarily decide, "We must go to monthly statements of contribution." Look at the practices of giving in your congregation and then make a wise, informed decision. Know this: many people under forty-five years of age are more likely to be helped by a monthly statement than by a quarterly statement. Think of your present congregation. Also, think of the people you hope to reach.

Take seriously the predominant economies and major giving practices with which people live as you:

- decide the timing of your giving development plan

- develop your mission budget for the coming year

- send statements of contributions

- nurture and encourage people as you share reports of giving progress across the year

When you take seriously where people are, you are more likely to grow the giving of your congregation.

Chapter 15

Enduring Gifts

People give enduring gifts this side of the river, not just as they cross over to the other side. People give enduring gifts in this lifetime. They also contribute enduring gifts generously through their estate.

In nearly every congregation there are people who want to share generously by means of enduring gifts. People want to be helpful in enduring ways. Thus, an important aspect of giving development is to make available the possibility of enduring giving among your congregation.

Whenever a congregation does not make this possibility available, does not open this "giving door," that simply means that the people in the congregation who want to be helpful in enduring ways will find other recipients—social service agencies, colleges, or universities—for their enduring gifts. The mission of your congregation will be greatly helped by providing the opportunity for people to share enduring gifts with your church. Of the six giving doors, this one is perhaps the least developed and understood.

The resources of this chapter will help expand your view. When a church focuses its enduring gifts program only on wills and legacies, it overlooks potential gifts from donors while they are yet alive. Consequently, it receives less than half of the monies people would give as enduring gifts.

I encourage you to a broader focus on enduring gifts than simply wills, legacies, and bequests. Allow people the opportunity to give enduring gifts during their lifetime as well as when they cross over the river.

Enduring gifts funds are a significant resource for the mission of a congregation. You can develop enduring gifts funds to assist your church in having solid financial resources. This will assist your church to deliver well nine out of the twelve central characteristics of an effective church.

Churches that do not deliver at least nine of the twelve central characteristics of effective churches tend to become declining or dying congregations, no matter what their finances. Some dying churches have been able to keep their doors open because they have monetary support from enduring gifts funds.

Regrettably, someone may claim the reason they are dying is because they have enduring funds. This is inaccurate. The reason they are dying is that for some time they have not delivered nine of the twelve central characteristics of an effective church. The enduring gifts have functioned as a safety net, providing a holding action. Without it, they would have died more quickly.

Enduring gifts help to provide life. The grapevine amplifies the few problems with which churches wrestle related to enduring gifts. We hardly ever hear of the many congregations with enduring gifts resources that quietly do excellent work year after year, decade after decade, in helping to advance God's mission.

The biblical text admonishes:

> Do not lay up for yourselves treasures on earth.
> (Matthew 6:10)

This text admonishes people who are preoccupied with laying up for themselves, in selfish, self-serving ways, treasures that minister only to their specific needs. The sin is focusing on ourselves. Focus on enduring gifts that have a missional, giving spirit of compassion, that will help people with their lives and destinies.

Some people say, "Trust in the Lord." That makes good sense. Yes, I encourage you to trust in the Lord. And sometimes God sends you someone who wants to share an enduring gift for the mission. Trust God then, as well. God provides resources sufficient unto the mission. Sometimes these resources come as enduring gifts.

Four steps will develop the enduring gifts potentially present within your congregation. These are:

- projects
- policies
- people
- possibilities

The first step is to plan the five to eight projects to be funded with the income from endowment giving.

Invite a task force to recommend the specific projects that will be helpful in advancing God's mission across the world. The best way for the task force to do this is to have broad-based discussions, looking for excellent ideas and good suggestions from among the grassroots of the congregations.

The more people who are invited to share their suggestions and longings, the more likely you are to discover the projects that match best with your church and community. This will also develop grassroots ownership and interest in enduring gifts. Balance, integrity, and broad-based appeal are the criteria that will help the task force select the best projects.

> Balance. Have a spirit of balance. Some projects will be for mission, some for mortar. Some projects would be for others, and some projects would be for your congregation. Some projects will be for programs, some for plant and facilities. It would be a grievous error to focus enduring gifts only on caring for the space and facilities of your own church. People will give only one-fourth of the money they would otherwise give. You need a genuine spirit of balance.

> Integrity. Select projects that have integrity and long-term value. Thus, for example, we would not have as an endowment project the building of a toolshed out back. We would not endow a project that has so narrow a focus that it might not have lasting value. You want projects that have an enduring character with flexibility and creativity for the future.

> Broad-based appeal. Think through, "What are the five to eight projects that will have the support of a wide range of

people in our congregation and our community?" Some people will have an interest in one, some in another. There will be a genuinely broad-based range of possibilities that will help people to discover their interest in enduring gifts.

Select a giving goal for each of the five to eight enduring gift projects. It is important that the goals be realistic and attainable. Stretching to reach a goal is good, yet it is unwise to set goals beyond one's capabilities. We are looking for goals that are reasonable and achievable.

Set the date when you hope to achieve each project's goal. You may have distinctive dates for each of the projects. One might be ten years from now; another, seven years; yet another, fifteen years. Select the date by which each project should be fully in place with enduring gifts.

When you have identified the projects, selected their goals, and set the dates, then compose a brief description of each project. Help those descriptions to be invitational and hopeful, concrete and compassionate. Give people the chance to know about the enduring gift projects, their goals and target dates. You will be amazed at how people come forward and contribute helpful, constructive, enduring gifts.

The primary reason most congregations do not receive enduring gifts is because they do not ask. They do not describe five to eight enduring gift projects. They do not have goals. They do not have target dates. You will find an amazing response once you have the projects well in place.

Some congregations have large numbers of memorial accounts—with $15 in one, $300 in another, $2,000 in another, $49 in another. This happens because there is no clear plan of what would help in enduring ways. So, when people are left to think up their own picture, the church ends up with thirty-seven random enduring gift accounts.

Develop five to eight major pictures of what will help in enduring ways. More than five to eight is too diffuse, too scattered. Certainly, it is appropriate to have a "general enduring gifts" project. Here people can give to the general endowment project fund, and that can be used in a wide range of ways. At the same time, people have the opportunity to give to the five to eight major pictures of enduring gifts that the congregation has developed.

The second step is to determine the policies by which the enduring gifts funds will be administered. There are four statements of policy that will help.

1. Gifts. It is helpful for you to have a policy as to how gifts are received and what procedures are followed by the enduring gifts team when a gift is received. Include policy guidelines that state the ways in which the giver is appropriately thanked.

2. Leadership. State clearly who will give leadership to the funds, describe how they will be administered, and identify the checkpoints that will ensure their wise development.

    Have a broad-based leadership team. Include people on this team who are leaders in the mission and program areas of the church and leaders in the grassroots life of the congregation. When only the church's trustees administer the enduring gifts funds, the regrettable stereotype develops that enduring gifts are primarily related only to space and facilities (trustees are seen to be property stewards).

3. Principal and interest. Have a policy that states that the principal will never be invaded. Assure potential and current givers that the principal will continue to have enduring value toward the mission of the church.

    On occasion, a congregation will have a policy that states that in any given year (for emergency purposes), the principal can be invaded by a certain percent. The problem with this is that when people see the principal being invaded, they direct their enduring gifts to other groups that do not invade the principal. By attempting to solve a short-term problem, a long-term loss of future enduring gifts is created.

Also, have a policy that the church cannot borrow from its enduring gifts funds. That is another form of invasion of the principal. Should the church not be able to repay the borrowed funds, it is unlikely that the endowment fund can collect from the church itself. The simplest policy is that the principal stay intact. This will encourage future giving.

Be certain to have a consistent policy in relation to the interest that each enduring gift fund earns each year. Be clear with potential givers as to what happens to the interest earned each year.

It may seem obvious that the interest will go toward the support of causes related to that specific enduring gifts project, but churches get into trouble by not having a consistent policy regarding what to do whenever some of the interest earned is left over and not used up by that year's project.

For example, one of the enduring gift funds might earn interest of $20,000 in a year. If only $12,000 of that is disbursed to advance that project during that year, $8,000 is unused. What happens to the $8,000? Where does it go? Plan ahead by stating policies to cover these contingencies. There are several possibilities, and you will think of others beyond these.

The $8,000 leftover interest is "saved." That is, it is kept in a separate account and is only available to be spent in coming years for causes related to that specific endowment project.

The leftover interest is added to the principal of that specific endowment fund, so that the principal grows as a result. Note: Some churches have the policy that a certain percentage of the interest must be put back into the principal each year as a hedge against inflation.

The leftover interest is added to the principal of the general endowment fund. The proponents of this policy suggest that the general endowment fund is the most flexible of all the funds, and it is important that it grow whenever possible.

The leftover interest is available for other needs that year beyond the designation of that endowment fund project.

You will think of other possibilities. My point is to encourage you to develop clear policies and stick with them consistently. As long as prospective givers know the procedures and policies, they are usually very happy to agree with them. What they do not respect—and have little tolerance for—is the feeling that the rules of the game change from one year to the next.

4. Grants. Describe how grants from the funds are shared. Are the grants available to committees from other churches or community agencies, or are they limited to use within your church? What are the simple procedures to apply for a grant from one of the enduring gift funds?

Share the policies as to how to request the grant, what specifics to include in a grant request, when the grant requests will be considered, how they will receive the grant, and what responsibilities they have to administer that grant in ways that match with their request and the approval thereof.

It is not the task of the enduring gifts leadership team to create the specific request to be funded each year. Their task is to respond graciously and affirmatively to responsible grant requests from committees, task forces, and teams of people. The enduring gifts team does not "possess" the enduring gifts funds. Rather, their task is to responsibly share grants initiated by groups in the congregations and, in some instances, the community. They act as good stewards of the funds entrusted to the church's enduring gifts program.

The policies related to gifts, leadership, principal and interest, and grants are appropriately developed in advance. Thus, future potential givers will have a clear understanding of how their gifts will be wisely used according to those policies.

One church—a medium-sized congregation—had received a major enduring gift twenty years before. There had been no policies or procedures written. There had not been five to eight projects available as enduring gift pictures. It is a wonder, even with their lack of preparedness, that they received this extraordinarily generous gift.

Regrettably, the donor died some months later without leaving instructions for the use of the gift. For twenty years the members of that congregation had argued over how that gift was supposed to be used. One friend "remembered" that the benefactor wanted the gift to support the space and facilities in enduring ways. Another friend of the family "remembered" that the gift was to be used for local missions. Another was not quite sure, but he thought it was intended to support the music program.

Their arguing and bickering—and that is precisely what they did for twenty years—cost them the loss of many other potential gifts they did not receive over those intervening twenty years. People who have an interest in giving enduring gifts simply do not give their gifts to congregations that wrangle and bicker over them. They say instead, "I think I will not give an enduring gift to the church; I'll give it to a university or college, the heart association, the cancer society . . . "

For that church, the solution was to put in place eight major enduring gift projects. Solid goals were set for each project. That initial major gift was used to seed each of the eight projects. The overall long-term goal became a goal four times the size of the initial major gift. The bickering stopped. They could focus on advancing their long-range enduring gifts program.

If you can think of several people who are perfectly capable of giving enduring gifts, the best way forward is to select five to eight major projects; decide policies that will be helpful; contact your potential givers and invite them to give generously. You can say, "Here are the suggested projects, and here are the policies we have developed to ensure a constructive, creative administration of enduring gifts that you give to the church."

The third step is to identify the people to serve as your enduring gifts leadership team. The following criteria will help your selection:

- Together, they are representative of the grassroots and the leadership of the congregations. This team of people includes more than the trustees, whose primary task is related to space and facilities.

- These people have the credibility and confidence of the congregation. They are trusted and respected. They are known as people of integrity by the congregation and the community. They are giving, compassionate leaders with the capacity to look at the whole.

- These people are leaders among the informal, relational networks present in the church and community. They have competencies in networking. They feel at ease in inviting people to consider giving an enduring gift.

- They have a long-term interest in one or more of the enduring gift projects and look forward to actively nurturing the achievement of the goal for one of the projects.

The fourth step is to help people know about the giving possibilities. You have decided the projects, developed the policies, and selected the team of people; now share the possibilities.

This last step is the opportunity for your team to help potential givers know how they can contribute enduring gifts. People give enduring gifts out of their present assets, their current income, and their estate. Create the spirit that you appreciate both modest and major enduring gifts. This is a grassroots effort, not solely a major gifts effort. Gifts of one dollar to one hundred thousand, and beyond, are equally appreciated.

One of the best ways to do this is to have an annual gathering of people in the congregation and the community (a covered-dish dinner or a banquet). The occasion should be one of good fun and good times, an occasion of rich, full community. At some point during the dinner, one person might briefly describe the five to eight enduring gift projects, announcing the gifts toward those projects that have been received during the past year and the amount remaining to reach the goal for each project. People who have given gifts during the past year might be personally thanked during the dinner.

Someone on the team might share a brief word confirming the continuity and consistency of the policies. Someone might invite people during the coming year to consider what God might be calling them to give generously as an enduring gift. One or two possibilities might be highlighted as ways that could help. Mostly, it would be a celebrative, memorable, annual gathering. You will be amazed at the way in which people will give enduring gifts to the mission of your church.

Over the years, I have had the privilege of helping a wide range of congregations develop their long-range plans. In many of these congregations, we have established an enduring gifts program.

Table 12 is an example of what one specific congregation in one specific community decided to do and what has been achieved to date. I encourage you to study it in order to benefit from this church's experience.

This example can help you as you design your own tailor-made enduring gifts program that matches with your own church and community. Your congregation may have three, five, or eight projects, rather than the seven of this church. The projects you select will be quite distinct from the ones here. The project goals and dates will suit your situation.

Please do not assume that by copying this example you can develop a successful program just like it. What works well in one church and in one community does not automatically work everywhere. I have shared it with you because I want you to have the benefit of seeing what it might look like. Study it and benefit from it.

How do you determine what goal to set for each enduring gifts project? First, determine the annual amount needed for that project. Then, based on a reasonable interest rate, determine how much principal you need in order to generate sufficient yearly income to meet that need.

Enduring Gift Project	Project Goal	Given	Yet to Be Given	Goal Date
Local and world missions	300,000	200,000	100,000	1999
Scholarships	100,000	100,000	Achieved	
Space and facilities	400,000	200,000	200,000	2004
Program development	200,000	100,000	100,000	2002
Music and worship	200,000	100,000	100,000	1998
Library resources	100,000	100,000	Achieved	
General	200,000		200,000	2008
Totals	*1,500,000*	*800,000*	*700,000*	

Table 12: Enduring Gifts Plan of One Congregation

Here is an example to help you with a space and facilities project. Discover the actual value of your buildings, not including the land. One to 3 percent of that value will be a reasonable rule of thumb as the annual amount to deliver preventative maintenance, ongoing restoration, and major emergency repairs for your space and facilities.

For example, let's say the value of your buildings (not including the value of the land) is $800,000. One percent is $8,000; 3 percent is $24,000. Depending upon the age of your buildings, the quality of their construction, the materials with which they were constructed, and the frequency of their use, it will take from $8,000 to $24,000 annually to achieve the necessary preventive maintenance, ongoing restoration, and major emergency repairs. If the buildings have a high frequency of use, plan on 3 percent. In the example shown in Table 12, $24,000 a year was needed. Thus, an endowment goal of $400,000 was established to provide continuing support for space and facilities care, based on an interest rate of 6 percent.

It is not reasonable to count on your annual budget to fund the week-to-week, month-to-month, year-to-year preventive maintenance, ongoing restoration, and major emergency repairs needed for most space and facilities. When churches draw from the annual budget to accomplish those purposes, two things happen.

First, and most often, the preventive maintenance and ongoing restoration are neglected; the building takes on a more and more faded and declining appearance. To remedy this, once every twenty-five years or so there is a capital funds drive to fix it up.

Second, the mission and outreach and the development of the life of the congregation are thereby limited and/or neglected.

It is wiser and less expensive to put in place an enduring gifts fund that would achieve this work.

The purpose of enduring gifts is to advance projects above and beyond those supported through the annual budget. The purpose of enduring gifts is not to subsidize or support the annual budget. In the example on space and facilities, the enduring gift fund does not pay for regular upkeep such as cleaning or lawn mowing. Those are appropriately the tasks of the annual budget. The enduring gift fund focuses on the larger issues of preventive maintenance, ongoing restoration, and major emergency repairs.

Likewise, an enduring gift fund to support music and worship will care for the tuning and maintenance of the piano and organ, the development of special seminars and events, and the underwriting of special musical programs. The annual budget delivers the day-to-day, week-to-week financial needs of the music and worship programs.

An enduring gifts fund to support future mission (and staffing for that mission) will support those new developments as pilot projects to advance specific mission possibilities in the community. Should these pilot projects become ongoing, their support might then be carried by the annual budget.

People want their lives to count in enduring ways. Develop enduring gifts to help people share their giving generously in long-lasting, enduring ways.

Conclusion

Conclusion

Chapter 16

Advancing Your Mission

Advance your mission; develop effective church finance practices. These two are good friends. The more you advance your mission, the more likely you are to develop effective church finances.

The more you develop healthy habits of effective church finances, the more likely you are to advance your mission. The two go hand in hand. They help one another. The more successful you are in one, the more successful you will be in the other.

Congregations that practice effective church finances keep first things first. They focus some of their very best creativity, leadership, and energies on advancing their mission. This focus on advancing their mission also helps them to develop healthy habits of church finances.

Congregations with solid practices of effective church finances have a better chance of doing effective mission. The one advances the other. Congregations with poor habits in church finances tend to do poorer in mission. Deficiency in the one drags down the other. Advance your mission; then develop your budget. Advance your mission; then raise your giving. Advance your mission; then set giving goals. Advance your mission; then grow your giving. Center on mission growth; then focus on budget growth. Keep first things first.

Habits of healthy church finances, at their best, are self-giving. When church finance is rightfully focused on giving development, it serves people. It helps people develop their capacity, their gift for giving. It is then that practices in church finances become self-giving, calm, and steady. The spirit becomes gracious and compassionate, invitational and hopeful. With integrity, the focus is on encouraging and nurturing people to grow forward the generosity of their giving.

At its worst, church finances can be self-serving. When church finance becomes preoccupied with institutional maintenance and survival, it becomes self-serving, nervous, and awkward. It becomes shrill and scolding, insistent and demanding. It loses its way.

When you center first on mission, you help to develop sound practices of church finances. Mission helps finance find the way.

Mission is more important than money. Some money is worth not raising. If raising it begets a maintenance mentality, it is not worth raising. If raising it creates a climate of scolding, law, and demand, then it is best left unraised. If raising it generates more ill will than goodwill, then one gains a little but loses much.

Some churches suffer from budget stress. They become stressed out over whether the budget is raised. They develop high anxiety over raising the funds and developing the budget. They push inordinately hard to raise that last 3 percent. They create more ill will than goodwill. They do not look to the long haul. They do not look four years ahead. They press for quick closure, immediate satisfaction, and short-term results.

One might ask:

What does it profit a church to raise its budget but lose its mission?

What does it profit a church to raise its budget but lose its goodwill?

It helps to keep the practices of effective church finances in their rightful perspective. Perspective prevents these tasks from becoming ends in themselves. Perspective helps them live out the mission.

Now, one cannot conclude that congregations that do not raise their budget are therefore in mission. They may not have much focus on mission at all; they simply may not know how to practice effective church finances. Failure to raise the budget cannot be taken as a sign of being in mission.

Effective church finances are a form of your mission. In a certain sense, the four areas of effective church finances live out mission. Healthy habits in church finances are practiced in these four areas:

- developing your budget
- raising your giving
- setting giving goals
- growing your giving

It is not that these areas are simply the means to mission. It is central that one go about these tasks in a missional way, with a missional spirit.

One cannot do these tasks in a maintenance mode of "business as usual"; then, somehow expect to switch from a maintenance mode to a mission focus. There is a strong reciprocal relationship between mission and church finances. When you practice healthy habits of church finances, you help to advance the spirit of the mission.

Whenever these tasks are done with a maintenance mentality, then what follows is done with that same mentality. The habit of maintenance—of "business as usual"—in developing your budget, raising your giving, setting giving goals, and growing your giving continues as the habit when the congregation tries to do mission. The mission is done with a maintenance mentality. Result: the mission withers.

When the four areas of effective church finances are carried out with a passion for mission, then what follows is a strong, healthy compassion for mission. The mission habit in church finances continues as the habit in mission. The mission grows forward in rich, strong ways.

One is consistent. When these tasks are done in a missional way, then one can count on them living out that mission. The way a church practices its finances teaches the theology they live.

A mission-driven congregation develops a mission-driven budget. And, note well, a mission-driven budget helps grow a mission-driven congregation. The two go hand in hand. Each helps the other.

An organizationally driven congregation develops an organizationally driven budget. An institutionally driven congregation develops an institutionally driven budget. The congregations that do the best in church finances have a rich, full, abiding compassion for mission. They are motivated by a theology of service, not a theology of survival. Their compelling, driving spirit is one of giving, serving, loving mission.

Effective church finances include solid, healthy practices and habits in:

- developing your budget
- raising your giving
- setting giving goals
- growing your giving

Decide how, in the coming four years, you can best advance and improve your habits in these areas in your congregation. Build your plan for effective church finance practices with these criteria in mind:

- competencies
- value in the community
- having fun
- promise for your future mission
- God's call for you

Think through your best competencies to grow forward healthy habits in the four areas of effective church finances. Do not focus first on the area that is weakest. Build on your strengths. Do better what you do best. Then you will be in the strongest position to tackle your weaknesses. When you begin with your weaknesses, you are in the weakest position to tackle your weaknesses.

Think through which of the four areas you are already doing reasonably well. Advance and improve them so they are in place with the strength of excellence.

Think through ways in which these four areas can have value in your community. Your congregation teaches the families within it certain attitudes and behavior patterns about life, giving, and money. Your church also teaches groups in your community a self-giving or a self-serving pattern of values.

Consider which of these areas you would have fun advancing first. Do not have a spirit that is onerous, worrisome, and depressing. Do not focus any more on doom and gloom. Select first the ones that you would genuinely have fun as leaders, pastors, and congregations advancing and improving.

Build these four areas in ways that have promise for the future mission of your congregation. Look ahead to the coming four years. Advance these areas in ways that will add to the momentum and dynamic of your mission. Pray that God will lead you. Ask God for wisdom and creativity. Seek sound, solid ways to grow these four areas of effective church finances in your congregation.

Giving is grace. The reward is the giving. As we give, we grow. We become newer, deeper people. Our sense of confidence and trust grows. Our sense of vision and hope grows. We live forward to our best true selves.

It is not "when you give, God will reward you." It is not that God "rewards" your giving. The reward *is* the giving. As you give, you share God's grace. The act of giving is virtually a sacrament of grace. The act of giving is both a sign and an event of the generosity of God in our lives. In this sense, the act of giving is the sharing of God's grace.

The giving is the grace. The grace is the giving. As you give, you share in God's grace. As you give, you discover the deeper resources for giving with which God has blessed you. It is not that the grace is "out there" somewhere. It is in you.

The event of giving is like the break of a new day, with the sun sharing its life-giving warmth. The event of giving is like a gentle rain that gives new life to the earth and all who dwell therein.

Giving is like the discovery of two friends that they love one another deeply and dearly. Giving has a warmth, a wonder, a grace about it. Giving is deeper than the oceans, higher than the mountains, more enduring than the earth. Giving is remembered long and well. Giving is its own reward.

Let prayer have a strong place in your fund-raising and budget development. Be constant in prayer. Rely less on gimmicks and gadgets, graphs and charts, tricks and trivialities, the latest fads and foolishness. These will come and go, rise and fall. They do not last.

Center yourself in prayer. Pray for the mission. Pray for the people. Pray that God will grant you wisdom and judgment, vision and common sense. Pray that God will help you to center on the mission and on the people.

Pray that God will save you from the dim distractions of maintenance and survival, institution and organization. Pray that God will keep you from demand and law. Pray that God will help you to invitation and grace.

Have a prayer life rich and full of grace, reverence and awe. Sense the wonder and mystery of God's grace. Be at peace. God is with us.

God gives us life for mission. We are given life to serve in mission. The purpose of life is mission, not simply existing. We live, move, and have our being that we might serve in mission. Life has purpose. We are not here for a fleeting moment and then gone. Life is not pointless. Life is not merely a momentary distraction. Life is not simply a series of empty events between the cradle and the grave.

Life is not some hollow shouting at the moon. Life is not one party after another, built on a superficial bravado that we only go round once. Life is not a shallow confidence in the fleeting flimsies of this world. God gives us life for mission.

God gives us mission for life. We are our most alive when we are in mission. Fulfillment is not found in consumerism. We have tried that path. We know its futility.

Fulfillment is found in what we build, not what we buy. With mission, there is an excitement, a fulfillment that comes in no other way. We have a genuine, abiding satisfaction that our lives matter for a great cause. We know we are living life at our best.

To be sure, mission is difficult, sometimes disappointing. There are moments of despair, depression, despondency. At the same time, people who are serving a great mission have the strong, confident sense that their lives count.

God gives us mission that we might have life. The text is clear.

Seek first the Kingdom. (Matthew 6:33; Luke 12:31)

Where mission happens, the Kingdom happens. Where events of reconciliation, wholeness, caring, and justice happen, there mission happens; there the Kingdom happens.

There is a direct correlation between mission and life.

We are given life to participate in the mission.

We find life in the mission.

May your life be rich and full. May your congregation grow even more healthy habits of church finance practices. May you advance your mission.

God bless you.

God be with your mission.

Index